P9-CFH-689

Education
and Work
for the Year
2000

Arthur G. Wirth

Foreword by Henry M. Levin

Education
and Work
for the Year
2000

CHOICES
WE FACE

Jossey-Bass Publishers · San Francisco

The second epigraph on the opening page of Chapter Twelve is reprinted with permission of Charles Scribner's Sons, an imprint of Macmillan Publishing Company, from *The God Within* by René Dubos. Copyright © 1972 by René Dubos.

For sales outside the United States, contact Maxwell Macmillan International Publishing Group, 866 Third Avenue, New York, New York 10022.

Manufactured in the United States of America.

The paper used in this book is acid-free and meets the State of California requirements for recycled paper (50 percent recycled waste, including 10 percent postconsumer waste), which are the strictest guidelines for recycled paper currently in use in the United States.

10% POST
CONSUMER
WASTE

Library of Congress Cataloging-in-Publication Data

Wirth, Arthur G.
    Education and work for the year 2000 : choices we face / Arthur G. Wirth
      p.   cm. — (Jossey-Bass education series)
    Includes bibliographical references and index.
    ISBN 1-55542-435-X
    1. Education—Economic aspects—United States. 2. Labor supply—United States—Effect of education on. 3. High technology and education—United States. 4. Educational change—United States. 5. Education—United States—Aims and objectives. I. Title. II. Series.
LC66.W57   1992
370'.973—dc20
                          92-11507
                              CIP

FIRST EDITION
HB Printing   10 9 8 7 6 5 4 3 2 1   *Code 9249*

The Jossey-Bass
Education Series

Contents

Foreword

One of the most common topics of the day is the search for answers to the question of how to create a productive work force that will enable the United States to compete with Japan, Germany, and other Asian and European countries. The conventional wisdom suggests that we need to raise student test scores to a level on par with those of students from the countries that are our economic competitors. This simple solution has become the dogma embodied in a wide range of reports by distinguished commissions on educational and economic policy, as well as in the policy actions that governments at all levels have undertaken.

By now the topic and its proposed solutions have become rather stale and uninspiring. Against this background, Arthur G. Wirth has made an invigorating and fresh contribution to the literature of this subject. Wirth's insights are important because he has the reputation of being a productive scholar who has spent a considerable portion of his career studying and writing about the connections between education and the world of work. In contrast to the prevailing pessimism about the future, Wirth is cautiously optimistic. He is visionary in an arena where most seek traditional palliatives for raising test scores. As well, he shows that emulating the Japanese is neither necessary nor likely to be a successful strategy. Instead, he talks about schools that will create thinking citizens who will be creative as well as productive and workplaces that will prize these traits.

Wirth is optimistic in a manner that is not consistent with existing trends. He argues against technocratic reforms that are premised on raising standardized test scores to successfully engage in global competition. Wirth maintains that standardized test goals are not only inadequate for the world of work that our children will enter, but they debase the educational system in a direction that becomes antilearning. Workers and citizens of tomorrow will need to be decision makers and problem solvers, to work effectively in teams, to engage in productive discourse, and to adapt to new learning situations. None of this is reflected in performance on standardized tests, and schools that teach to these tests will prepare workers for rapidly evaporating assembly-line positions rather than for the opportunities of tomorrow.

Wirth points out that the future productivity of the labor force rests as heavily on the organization of the workplace as it does on the organization of the school. Japanese automobile producers have been as successful in the efficient production of high-quality cars in the United States as they have been in Japan. Their U.S. operations build very heavily on extensive investments in worker training and on commitments to continuing worker employment and emphasize team production, collaboration, and problem-solving skills. Most importantly, their U.S. employees have never experienced Japanese schools, so their success cannot be attributed to Japanese schooling magic.

Wirth proposes an educational system that gets both students and teachers actively involved in inquiry. If we want our students to be problem solvers, we must get them into schools where students take responsibility for making critical decisions and obtaining problem-solving experiences. The same is true for teachers and other school staff. Parents must become active participants in this endeavor, and schools need to support parental involvement. All of his suggestions for remediation address schools that connect classroom learning with real-world experiences and that build on strong teamwork and communications skills. It is democracy rather than technocracy that is at the heart of transformation of both schools and workplaces. Wirth provides examples of transformed workplaces and transformed schools throughout the book to illuminate this theme.

Arthur G. Wirth gives us a vision of a desirable future and convinces us that it is within our reach if we have the will. Beyond that, he provides us with practical insights and illustrations to point out the steps that we need to take. The stakes are high. It is not only our future economy that is at stake, but our future democracy as well. Wirth has given us a framework for addressing both through a revitalized educational and industrial system. It should be must reading for both economic and educational policymakers and informed laypersons.

June 1992

Henry M. Levin
*Professor of Education
and Economics
Stanford University*

To
South High School, Columbus, Ohio,
whose teachers introduced
working-class pupils like myself
to the world of books and ideas
(1933–1936)

Preface

I have been involved in the study of the relations between education and work for the past fifteen years. This interest grew out of my teaching "Alternative Philosophies of Work" in the Human Resource Management Program and "Philosophies of Education" in the Department of Education at Washington University.

A word about why I decided to write this book. As America entered the 1990s, it was clear that we were well into a new postindustrial era marked by the computer/communications revolution, a competitive world market, and serious ecological damage. American work and schooling were struggling to cope with these revolutionary changes and came under heavy criticism. In the struggles of the early nineties, I saw the possibility of developments that could strengthen both institutions and help us achieve a better quality of life. But there were weighty obstacles and resistance as well. By writing about both the promise and the obstacles, I hope to improve our chances of capitalizing on a propitious moment.

I elaborate on all of this in the following chapters. The

gist of the argument, however, is this: The centralized control style of scientific management that once dominated industrial-era work—and had spilled over to influence schools—was becoming dysfunctional for meeting the turbulent change of the computer/electronic era. Some leaders in industry and education were beginning to recognize that we need alternatives to bureaucratic centralism in order to be more creative in dealing with rapid change. One alternative is to combine certain values from our democratic tradition with the power of electronic technology. Behind the gloom of the daily news, I see this development as opening exciting prospects—prospects that could simultaneously increase our strength and viability while leading us toward more humane living.

I wrote this book to explore this idea and lend my support to certain promising trends. They *need* support because nothing less than the locus of power is at issue, and those who are comfortable with the status quo will resist.

Overview of the Contents

Chapter One, "Introduction: A Crisis of the Human Spirit," establishes the fact that we are confronted with revolutionary changes—above all, an electronically driven technological revolution, a competitive global market, and dangerous ecological damage. In meeting the challenges, we are pulled by two value traditions: a bureaucratic, centralized control tradition versus the tradition of democratic ideals. In education, an initial wave of reform in the 1980s focused on centrally controlled test score accountability. Its failure was followed by a second reform effort—school restructuring based on more democratic values. In the 1990s, therefore, we are torn by a dilemma: Which tradition should be given priority as work and education are being transformed by computer technology?

Chapter Two, "Americans in School: Teaching and Learning Under Duress," shows the debilitating effects on teachers of the centralized control pressures of test score accountability: the violation of professional autonomy and integrity, the demoralization of caring, creative teachers. This chapter offers counterexamples of how such teachers want to teach, and it points to underlying philosophical issues.

Chapter Three, "Americans at Work: Architects or Bees?," shows how key segments of industry in the 1980s, in order to cope with complex change, were relinquishing the controls of scientific management and moving toward participative, democratic, sociotechnical design of work. It shows the growing need for a better-educated, flexible work force capable of continuous learning.

Chapter Four, "The Japanese Model: Can It Work for Us?," demonstrates that when we perceive the Japanese as making superior efforts in industry and education we tend to look to them as a model for answers. It offers examples of Japanese effectiveness—including the ability to win the voluntary commitment of individuals to the welfare of groups—but it shows that Japanese techniques are grounded in the Bushido philosophy of Japanese culture, which cannot be transferred to the United States. We have to find answers in the strengths of our own cultural traditions.

Chapter Five, "The Choice We Face: Automate or Informate?," argues that in order to meet the challenge of electronically driven change we are already beginning to create American answers for effective performance in high-tech industry—answers that integrate democratic values with computer technology. The chapter centers on two insightful analyses of the choices we confront: Shoshanna Zuboff says we must choose to "automate" or "informate"; Robert Reich explains why the skills and attitudes of symbolic analysis are crucial for both new work and new education.

Chapter Six, "The Business Perspective on Schooling: A Mixed Message," shows how insightful American leaders of high-tech industries recognize that old-fashioned scientific management controls must be replaced by democratic sociotechnical work design. They recognize the need for parallel changes in school structures and learning styles, but the business control tradition leads them to accept such changes only if they can produce bottom-line results on national testing.

This condition brings teachers under centralized controls that inhibit creativity in the classroom.

Chapter Seven, "Testing: Cure or Curse?," portrays testing as one of the most complex and troubling aspects of school improvement efforts. On the one hand, communities have a right to know if effective learning is occurring. On the other, bureaucratic mass testing can corrupt the integrity of teaching and learning and drive creative teachers out of the profession. This chapter describes efforts at designing alternative forms of testing—and the problems that attend them. It points out the direct correlation of test scores with family income—and the dishonesty involved in asking for improved scores while ignoring the effects of increasing poverty, family disintegration, and inequitable school financing.

Chapter Eight, "Restructuring: New Strategies for Learning," describes features of the second wave of reform that emerged as America entered the nineties. The failure of 1980s reform by top-down prescription led to a countermove to restructure schools that embodied more participative styles of school management and active, constructivist styles of student learning. This chapter shows how these efforts are hampered by deepening poverty and inequalities.

Chapter Nine, "The Issues in Science Education," recognizes that competence in science is critical for a society being transformed by science and computer technology. This chapter illustrates how the debate over science education reflects the parallel tension between the "automating" and "informating" options in industry and the first and second waves of reform in education.

Chapter Ten, "Computers in the Schools: What Do We Do with Them?," explains how different strategies for computer use in schools also reflect the tension between usage that is of a routinized "automating" type and that which is participatory "informating." The Apple Classrooms of Tomorrow (ACOT) program, discussed at length, represents an example of the second approach.

Chapter Eleven, "Vocational Education: An Instrument for Educational Transformation?," shows how changes in

the world's work are affecting thinking about occupational
education. We face great changes due to the impact of computerization on work as well as the shifting nature of the
work force—including the special problems of impoverished
minorities. The chapter explains how the Carl D. Perkins
Vocational and Applied Technology Education Act Amendments of 1990 open new perspectives on the issues of integrating high school and community college programs and using
occupational studies as a strategy for a liberalizing reform of
secondary education.

Chapter Twelve, "Education and Work in the Year
2000: Capitalism with a Human Face?," reviews earlier
themes. It emphasizes Robert Reich's argument that to meet
challenges of electronic postindustrialism we need the skills
of symbolic analysis in work and learning: abstraction, system
thinking, experimental inquiry, and collaboration. These
views coincide with Shoshanna Zuboff's case for the "informating" strategies. Although one can cite examples from the
"restructuring" wave of educational reform in the early 1990s
that would support this orientation, the growth of poverty is
a major impediment. We have two choices: Enter the twenty-
first century with the handicap of an economically divided
society, or promote a "high democratic society" in which we
teach all of our young the skills of symbolic analysis that can
make them viable in the world market—and might also equip
them with values to reduce violence toward nature and each
other.

Audiences and Uses

This book offers a perspective on the complex changes going
on in American work and schooling as we make decisions for
meeting global challenges of the new postindustrialism. It
identifies the parallel value choices we face in both institutions and argues for options that combine democratic values
with the power of computer technology.

The book is relevant for a variety of university courses
that are concerned with institutions confronting dramatic

social change. This holds for courses I have taught in such areas as educational policy issues, philosophy of education, school and society, and curriculum and instruction. Moreover, its content is relevant for courses in human resource management and for programs in science/technology/society. For those in vocational or occupational education, it shows the broad forces that are forcing a rethinking of the style and content of vocational studies.

Since few social concerns for the 1990s are more important than the redesign of work and schooling, the book is relevant too for the general public. There is much here as well for leaders of industry and labor who see the urgent need for rethinking the nature of education-work relations. Moreover, it has important relevance for educators in general and their professional organizations: the National Education Association, the American Federation of Teachers, the Vocational Education Association, and others.

My general goal is to show a variety of policymakers how the choices between "automating" or "informating" in industry have profound meaning for key aspects of schooling—aspects like testing, programs for at-risk children, the use of computers, science education, the relation of vocational to liberal studies, and restructuring.

Acknowledgments

One of the most satisfying experiences in bringing a study like this to a close is reflecting on the many whose contributions made it possible. In the far past are the teachers in the working-class schools of the German Village in Columbus, Ohio, who first opened my mind in the 1930s to the world of books and ideas. Having been introduced to the life of the mind, I eventually encountered the myriad authors whose insights made this book possible.

I have profited in many ways from the stimulation and challenge of colleagues and students at Washington University. I am especially grateful to Bryce Hudgins, chair of the Department of Education, who made available the office and secretarial help that have made it possible for me to continue my intellectual interests as an emeritus professor.

My longtime colleagues and mentors, Raymond E. Callahan and Louis Smith, read the manuscript with care and, as always, raised the questions and comments I needed to hear. I am indebted also, for careful readings of the text in whole or in part, to my colleagues Kathi Beyer, Timothy Lensmire, and Elliott Seif. David Dwyer, project director and principal scientist for Apple Computer, Inc., generously made available research writings on the Apple Classrooms of Tomorrow (ACOT) project and led me through ACOT sites in Cupertino, California, and Columbus, Ohio. Larry Rosenstock, director of the Rindge School of Technical Arts, and Arthur Steinberg of the Massachusetts Institute of Technology made available to me their important thinking and work on vocational and occupational education.

At the Work Research Institutes in Norway, Jon Fröde Blickfeldt, Max Elden, and Philip Herbst generously guided me to the writing and work sites where the exciting concepts of democratic sociotechnical work theory are being developed.

John Pingree, nonpareil typist of manuscripts, continually amazed me by his patience and skill in preparing numerous drafts of the text. I also wish to thank Lesley Iura and Frank Welsch, editors at Jossey-Bass, who guided me through the stages of book preparation.

Finally, I appreciate the generosity of Marilyn Cohn, Robert Kottkamp, Rita Roth, and Elliott Seif, who permitted me to draw on aspects of their research and writings. I thank the editors of *Dissent* for permission to quote copyrighted material and the editors of *The Teachers College Record, Educational Studies,* and *The Journal of Thought,* who permitted me to quote from my own articles that had appeared in their journals.

St. Louis, Missouri　　　　　　　　　　　　　Arthur G. Wirth
June 1992

The Author

Arthur G. Wirth received his B.A. (1940), M.A. (1941), and Ph.D. (1949) degrees in the philosophy of education, all from Ohio State University. He taught at the Ohio State University Laboratory School (1947-1949), at Brooklyn College (1949-1961), and at Washington University (1961-1985). He became professor emeritus in 1985. At Washington University, he taught courses in the social foundations of education, the philosophies of education, and alternative philosophies of work in the interdisciplinary Human Resource Management Program.

In the 1980s, Wirth received grants from the John Dewey Foundation that enabled him to visit Work Research Institutes in Norway and Sweden, where democratic sociotechnical work theory and practice were being developed. He has studied similar work situations in various parts of the United States.

He is the author of numerous articles. Among his books are *John Dewey as Educator* (1966), *Education in the Technological Society* (1973), and *Productive Work in Industry and Schools* (1983). He was editor of the John Dewey Society Lecture Series (Harper & Row) from 1959 to 1967.

One

Introduction: A Crisis of the Human Spirit

Education keeps pace with the life and growth of the community, and is altered both by changes imposed on it from without and by transformations in its internal structure and intellectual development. And, since the basis of education is a general consciousness of the values which govern human life, its history is affected by changes in the values current within the community.

—Werner Jaeger (1945)

American work and education now confront the challenge of a series of interconnected global changes: the computer/electronic revolution that is pushing us into a postindustrial society, the emergence of a competitive global market, and an ecological crisis resulting from our careless treatment of the natural and human environments. The kind of responses we make to this order of complexity is affected by the struggle between two value traditions in American culture. Essentially, it is a struggle between the scientific efficiency tradition in industry and schools versus the need to combine values from our democratic tradition with high technology to cope with the turbulent change of the electronic era.

I write because I think the 1990s offer us a unique opportunity to revitalize the more humane, democratic values of American culture. This is so for the practical reason that these values, when combined with new technology, give us our most effective power for meeting the challenges of the electronic era. It will not be easy, however, for it means relinquishing the centralized control habits that gave us industrial-

1

era dominance in the first three-quarters of this century. It means making a second major cultural change within the hundred-year period just ending. In the 1890s we were moving rapidly from a rural, small town America to an urban, corporate industrial society. In the 1990s we will be moving swiftly from factory industrialism to computer-driven, global postindustrialism.

A central feature of corporate industrialism was the efficiency of scientific management created by the engineer genius Frederick W. Taylor. Taylorism was the system of technocratic control designed to discipline an ill-educated, immigrant work force whose energies were to be welded to the relentless rhythms of assembly-line production. It was a system in which thinking and authority were reserved for technical/managerial experts who broke production into minute prescribed tasks, while people at work were reduced to programmed performance under supervision. It was the hierarchical, bureaucratic control system that Max Weber held to be inevitable under mass industrialism. Although we mastered it with great effectiveness, its manipulative hierarchical style conflicted with such values as the equal worth and dignity of persons, the chance to participate as an active subject rather than a mere object, the chance to use one's distinctive capacities to learn, think, and grow. It was at odds in a fundamental way with the tradition of democratic values.

By this last decade of the twentieth century, evidence is mounting that centralized Taylorist efficiency is rapidly becoming dysfunctional for meeting challenges of the new era. I shall argue that a new style of leadership—one that combines participative values with computer technology—can make us more competitive by releasing creativity and, in addition, improve the quality of life in work and schools. But it will be contentious, too, because it involves a change in the nature and locus of power.

In the chapters that follow I offer a perspective on the tension between these two conceptions for the design of work and education. One way to schematize the theme is to consider Shoshanna Zuboff's concepts of "automate" versus "informate" as metaphors for the broad choices we face. Zuboff, a professor in the Department of Organizational Behavior at Harvard's Business School, made intensive studies of the emerging design of work in high-tech industries. In her book, *In the Age of the Smart Machine: The Future of Work and Power,* she cited two strategies for linking human components with electronic technology: an "automating" strategy and an "informating" strategy.

Automating extends Taylorist technocratic assumptions of the industrial era to high-tech conditions. It assumes that technical experts are best qualified to harness the power of technology to get work done. They retain centralized control over the information required to make decisions about the design of technology, the behavior of people at work, and the solutions to problems that arise. This automating style of controlling work supports the value and needs of the hierarchical, bureaucratic efficiency tradition.

The informating strategy challenges the bureaucratic control model on the grounds that it is not flexible enough to meet the challenges of the computer/communications revolution. It fails because its fixation on control prevents it from tapping higher human capacities for communicating, collaborating, creating novel solutions, and making value judgments. The informating strategy gives people in the workplace access to relevant information so they can become active agents in troubleshooting, suggesting innovations, and making decisions. While the informating strategy may be chosen for reasons of functional efficiency alone, its style in work and learning provides a framework for people to experience participatory, creative values of the democratic tradition. What is really at issue in this use of metaphors is the quality of life and learning that can be experienced *within* the institutions of work and learning. We are not talking about political democracy as majority vote for control of the enterprise itself.

We need to recognize, however, that American industrial designers are motivated primarily by practical concerns when they move in the participatory informating direction rather than by the desire to strengthen democratic values. The motivation is simple: the desire to cope more effectively with the competitive global challenges of the computer age. As a positive consequence, we may be forced to the strengths of our better nature for utilitarian reasons. As maverick economist Hazel Henderson put it, "For the first time in history morality has become pragmatic."[1] That is not all bad, since people are powerfully motivated by the need for survival. But there is a downside in relying on narrow utilitarian grounds. A shallow commitment can falter quickly in the face of unavoidable problems or shifts in the fickle winds of fashion.

This is why I think it is time to acknowledge that, behind this debate, there is a deeper matter at stake. Michael Harrington articulated it throughout his *Politics at God's Funeral:* The crisis of our time is the crisis of the human spirit, and we have to give up the illusion that we can talk adequately about the real problems of our lives and our work by using only the bland language of technocratic reform.

This message was reconfirmed and expanded by Vaclav Havel as he wrote *Living in Truth* during the crumbling of East European communism. Havel wrote that the fundamental challenge in both corporate capitalism and party/state communism is to resist everywhere "the irrational momentum of anonymous, impersonal inhuman power—the power of ideologies, systems, *apparat,* bureaucracy, artificial languages. . . . The question is . . . whether we shall succeed in . . . rehabilitating the personal experience of human beings as the initial measure of things . . . , in making human community meaningful, in returning content to human speaking, in reconstituting, as the focus of all human action, the autonomous, integral and dignified human." It really is not all that important, he says, "whether, by accident or domicile, we confront a Western manager or an Eastern bureaucrat in this very modest and yet globally crucial struggle against the momentum of impersonal power." What is important is the struggle "to live in dignity and partnership."[2]

We are at a point where the price of bureaucratic control that forces us to live contrary to our deeper human self-interest is simply too high. In January 1987 at the Meadow-creek Project, Fox, Arkansas, I heard Langdon Winner, author of *The Whale and the Reactor,* say: "The underlying issue is to create an ontology of ourselves that preserves our essential qualities of dignity, integrity, creativity, that we won't permit technology to violate."

Since I believe that Shoshanna Zuboff's automating/ informating argument is useful for clarifying the critical choices in work and schooling, I shall examine her ideas more systematically in Chapter Five, together with related concepts from Robert Reich's *The Work of Nations: Preparing Ourselves for 21st Century Capitalism.* Reich argues that survival depends on employing the collaborative skills of symbolic analysis in both work and schooling—and that we are not moving nearly as rapidly in that direction as the times require.

Meanwhile, several caveats: First, I use Zuboff's auto-mating and informating as metaphors rather than as neat formulas to which events in work or schooling are to be compared in detail. Second, in no way do I assume that because the informating organizational style seems fruitful it is there-fore inevitable. I do not assume a sudden benevolence on the part of corporate leadership, grounded in faith in democratic values, that motivates them to move in this direction. If the informating option is chosen it will be because of hardheaded conclusions that it is essential for competitive survival and profit. The traditional assumption in industry has been that democratic values have no relevance for corporate function-ing: Democracy should be confined to periodic voting in polit-ical elections. Yet democratic values may well be seen as having an important role in the design of work and learning under the new postindustrial conditions.

This book represents a return to themes I first treated in *Productive Work in Industry and Schools: Becoming Persons Again* (1983). As an educator in the late 1970s, I was struck by the fact that the two key institutions of work and school-ing were confronted by productivity problems, but they were responding in quite different ways. A tiny sector of management that had never considered democracy as relevant or legitimate to its functioning was now, under the Japanese threat, exploring the need for collaborative values and techniques in the workplace. Educational policymakers, who had long argued for linkages of democracy and education, were now charging ahead with bureaucratic, technical, efficient "reform."

As an educator, I began following the parallel developments in both institutions in the late seventies when I saw the decline of teacher morale in the face of the campaign for test score accountability. The movement was committed to the principle that the only thing that counts is what can be counted. It was an expert-driven movement aimed at treating school learning as a measurable production function with teachers expected to improve bottom-line numbers on test scores. The most creative, committed teachers, violated by this reductionist chopping of learning into measurable fragments of knowledge, were becoming demoralized or quitting. Others were cheating. This seemed crazy. Since this technical efficiency model was coming from the Taylorist tradition in industry, I wanted to see if anyone in industry thought it was crazy. This led to travels to experimental industrial situations in Scandinavia and the United States where I found a new concept of work design being created: democratic sociotechnical work theory. The proponents accused the technical efficiency tradition of being guilty of the "technical fix" error— the assumption that all problems lend themselves to expert-designed technical solutions. This orientation ignored the "socio" dimension of human work: the capacity for communicative, reflective, collaborative troubleshooting and inventiveness. To ignore an essential aspect of human work is to be out of touch with reality (that is, crazy).

The democratic sociotechnical involvement was in its infancy in the United States as we entered the 1980s. Coming into the 1990s provided an opportunity to gain perspective on what had been happening in the past ten years in the two institutions. In industry, under the press of foreign competition, there was a continued but sporadic movement toward workplace democracy. In education, one could see that that decade had been marked by two waves of school reform. The first wave, dominant in the Reagan administration, was the effort to get "excellence" by controlling educators with test score accountability. At the opening of the Bush administration, the new secretary of education, Lauro Cavazos, declared that top-down expert-decreed reforms had failed. With a growing recognition of that failure came a second wave of reform—a loosely defined demand for "restructuring" with features like local school autonomy, respect for teachers' initiatives, respect for the individuality of children, and calls for active "constructivist" learning to replace passive linear styles. In other words, in America's workplaces and schools, values of the democratic tradition were getting more attention because of the breakdown of centrally controlled efficiency styles.

The realities of electronic postindustrialism may push us toward the values of our better selves. But there is the contrary possibility that the automating option—combining centralized expert control with computer technology—will prevail. In the chapters that follow I explore the tension between these contending forces. I do this with examples from the worlds of work and schooling—and with an eye, I hope, to "the crisis of the human spirit," which involves the way people will experience their lives in these two key institutions. John Dewey said in 1916, as he viewed the awesome impact on American life of the early corporate, factory industrialism, "Democracy has to be born anew in each generation, and education is its midwife."[3]

Two

Americans in School: Teaching and Learning Under Duress

Mike Cooley, president of the British Union of Engineers, one sunny morning on the banks of the Thames, gave me this quote from a book he was writing:

> Either we will have a future in which human beings are reduced to a sort of bee-like behavior, reacting to the systems and equipment specified for them; or we will have a future in which masses of people, conscious of their skills in both a political and technical sense, decide that they are going to be the architects of a new form of technological development which will enhance human creativity and mean more freedom of choice and expression rather than less. The truth is we shall have to make the profound decision whether we intend to act as architects or bees.[1]

The choice between architect or bee confronts us in American schools and work alike. It is true that the bee-like way of treating teachers and students in schools came from American industry. Yet, ironically, during most of the 1980s the chances of shifting toward the architect side seemed to be better in industry than in the schools.

The Violation of People at Work in Schools

This chapter is about the work of teachers and how it was violated by the first wave of educational reform: test score accountability. The phrase "violation of people" refers to the behavior of institutions that violate our dignity and treat us like bees. Ernest Becker in *The Structure of Evil* helped me to see that. Becker pointed out that since the rise of science and the Enlightenment in the seventeenth and eighteenth centuries we have been confronted by two major images of humans: *l'homme machine* (the human as mechanism) and *homo poeta* (humans as meaning makers). The Newtonian image of the world as a physical mechanism moving according to mathematically regulated laws of force and motion gave powerful support to the notion that humans are manipulable objects within the grand mechanical design. That view was captured nicely by the eighteenth-century philosopher Julien Offray de la Mettrie in his phrase *l'homme machine*. The problem with that concept, according to Becker, is that it violates our deeper needs as *homo poeta*. We create structures of evil, Becker says, whenever we create institutions that deny people the opportunity to act in the world creatively as meaning makers.[2] In our time, such institutions are not only immoral; they are also impractical because our chance of resolving the problems of turbulent change in a momentous transition period depends on utilizing the full range of our creative strengths as *homo poeta*.

With our own children, we learned that the best bet for getting our kids hooked on learning was to have them with teachers who worked from what the Greeks had called their *entheos*, the personal god within that is the source of *enthusiasmos* or enthusiasm. Such teachers could teach creatively—as *homo poeta*—and get their pupils learning active-

ly as meaning makers. If the new reductionist emphasis—
"teaching is teaching for tests"—did damage to that end,
and in addition taught children that adults will cheat when
fearful and resentful, then something crazy and crazy-making was going on.

As test score pressures increased on teachers, I made
efforts to find statements by teachers who could articulate
what was happening to their work and what they *wanted* to
happen. Here I report on statements by the Boston Women's
Teachers' Group and the National Council of Teachers of
English in their *Report Card on Basal Readers.*

First, there is the material from the research study by
the Boston Women's Teachers' Group, *The Effect of Teaching on Teachers.*[3] The study was based on in-depth, fifteen-
hour interviews of twenty-five women elementary school
teachers over a two-year period. About half of them had
taught for fifteen years, the other half less. They were
selected to match substantially the national teacher population in terms of socioeconomic and racial background, mar-
ital status, educational attainment, and father's occupation
within the limitations of the small sample. They had taught
in impoverished urban schools as well as in affluent systems.
Lengthy analyses of the data over many months led the
researchers to conclude that teachers' feelings with regard
to burnout, isolation, job satisfaction, and sense of efficacy
were rooted in the *working relations* and *institutional structures* of the schools. In their words: "Teacher stress is an
institutionally derived problem, not a result of individual
personality failures, as teachers have been led to believe." I
can only sketch a profile here of what they found. Since the
study illustrates what I call "crazy-making" and "violation
of people," I shall make a rough sort according to these
categories. They are not unrelated.

First, "crazy-making." This phrase, from Old Norwegian *krasa,* refers to that which is crushed or fragmented or
out of reach with reality. In the following passages I indicate
whether each statement is a commentary by the researchers or
a teacher's statement:

Researcher Commentary: Teachers work in an institution which holds, in its rhetoric, that questioning and debating, risk and error, develop one's thinking ability. But learning situations are structured to lead to one right answer, and both teachers and students are evaluated in ways that emphasize only quantifiable results.

Teacher: The worst thing is that you get this printout and you're expected to find the profile of each individual child and then find material on those specific skills that they have to master . . . and then they take a multiple choice test where they have to choose a, b, or c. Well, the kids glance at the choices and figure out that one of those endings makes a pretty good answer. They never read the whole sentence. They're used to a world of filling blanks without it meaning anything. I mean it's meaningless work.

Teacher: This year my principal's evaluation said this: "Five kids looked up from their work and looked out of the window within a five-minute period. Now if you multiply five kids and five minutes in a period and you place it in an hour you get the percentage who are not doing their work and not involved."

Massachusetts is not alone in imposing this style. Deborah Meier, director of the Central Park East Secondary School in New York City, reports how evaluators prescribed hundreds of specific written goals. Example: "Given teacher supervision, praise, and positive reinforcement, the student will attend to difficult assignments for five minutes, three times out of four as recorded by teacher."[4] Now, I ask, who's crazy?

And now some commentary pointing to violation of persons as *homo poeta:*

Researcher Commentary: Teachers were continually perplexed by the admonition to be *professional* while the area in which their expertise could be applied became narrower and narrower. Teacher: "The thing that aggravates me is that we as educators are not treated as adults. . . . They check up on you like you're children. . . . They walk into your room and you have to be within minutes of where your program card says."

Teacher: Every Tuesday is a half day for faculty meetings. . . . People sit there deadpan because they don't want to commit themselves, you know, get themselves into any kind of hot water. Most of the stuff comes down from the central office that is really separate from the actual core of teaching.

Teacher: One of the things that has bothered me about the hurried pace of teaching today is that a lot of the creativeness is taken away from you—the feeling that I'm going to think of a new, fresh way to do it. The curriculum gets reduced to: "Here is a book and teach it. You should be on page 200 by such and such a date." It has nothing to do with your kids and nothing to do with whatever ideas you might want to bring in.

Teacher: I think the merit evaluation is even worse than seniority. Oh, my God. In this particular school it has destroyed any type of relations. I mean you look at the person next door to you and you say, "Gee, I wonder how many points she has." So instead of encouraging teachers to be more open about what they're doing, there isn't one bit of sharing. When you're in competition with another person for your job, you're pitting one person against another. I think in this business you can't do that. Because we tell the kids that everybody is unique.

Teacher: I started seeing myself not taking the risks I used to. I used to do all kinds of interesting things with my students—build things all over the classroom. But every once in a while someone would notice that the classroom wasn't as neat as it should be . . . and since anything can be pointed to, you start to retrench. You feel a lack of growth and you look around. And I decided to leave.

This teacher left. For those who stay there are heavy pressures to yield to the technocratic rationale:

Researcher Commentary: The teacher, under attack for failing to help children reach arbitrary grade-level goals, accedes to the greater wisdom of the commercial test makers and the research academics. Once started on the road to quantification, the method becomes addictive.

The new *objective* type of teacher evaluations that have been introduced into the schools are examples of such quantitative methods. They take great pains to code and enumerate the type, number, and direction of the interactions of the teacher with her pupils within the classroom.

The more quantitative measures and national exams are used to evaluate the teacher, the more she will feel the need to use such quantitative methods to judge her students and other teachers. She is now the in-class representative of the national norms and country-wide bell curves. Once she has entered the child's progress into her book, both she and her pupils are assumed to be easily understood and evaluated.

The same factors work on students. There is John Goodlad's famous observation that not even 1 percent of the instructional time in classes is devoted to discussion that "required some kind of open response involving reasoning or perhaps an opinion from students . . . the extraordinary degree of student passivity stands out."[5] An example was furnished to me by Rita Roth from her observation journal:

Teacher: Why aren't you doing your work, Alphonse?

Alphonse: I thought we were going to read today.

Teacher: That's what we did—you just had reading group.

Alphonse: But I thought we would read today.

Teacher: We just did, Alphonse. We looked for "s" sounds in your book, did two "s" sheets in your workbook, and here is the worksheet you should be doing right now to find some more "s" words.

Alphonse: But I thought we would read today, you know, *READ read.*[6]

Deborah Meier's comment on the parallel experience of New York City teachers once more is relevant: "Predictable multiple-choice questions replaced *conversation* about books. Reading scores went up, literacy collapsed. . . . Improved test scores, alas, are best achieved by ignoring real reading activity."[7]

I have talked with many teachers who feel unable to articulate what is wrong with the model being forced on them. It seems so reasonable. An applicant to a medieval shoemakers' guild would be told: "You say you are a shoemaker—make a shoe." In a twentieth-century culture obsessed with bottom-line results it is assumed that reading teachers can be made accountable by simply telling them to "show us your reading score results." What possibly can be wrong with that?

The issue, says Denis Goulet, Notre Dame professor of government, is not whether one is for or against efficiency, but what *kind* of efficiency for human institutions? Western engineering-type efficiency, which worked wonders in closed mechanical systems by simple quantitative measures of inputs to outputs, can be dangerous to well-being in nonmechanical human systems. What we now need, says Goulet, is to explore ways of becoming *integrally efficient:* how to produce efficiently while optimizing social and human values.[8] Integral efficiency would tell us that if we are teaching so that scores are going up but real reading is going down, we ought to stop it because it is inefficient.

The Basals: Dominant But Dead

One would expect wide agreement with the contention that we ought to stop whatever is causing real reading to go down. But as late as 1988 the Commission on Reading of the National Council of Teachers of English (NCTE) was moved to write a blistering report on what was happening to their work: *Report Card on Basal Readers.* Indeed, it motivated me to write an article, "The Basals—'Dominant But Dead' vs. Gadamer and Language for Hermeneutic Understanding," clarifying the rationale behind the dominant controlling use of "the basals" and why teachers were resisting.[9] But I also attempted to show how two contrasting approaches reflect different philosophical images of human nature and learning—using Michel Foucault's analysis to show the historical roots of the intrusion of rational control into modern institutions and Hans-Georg Gadamer to show an alternative image of humans as *homo poeta*. They point to issues we ought to confront in considering the quality of life and learning in our schools.

The Report Card on Basal Readers (1988) of the NCTE calls the basals the paradigm of test-driven instruction in U.S. elementary education;[10] the basal readers became the model for the texts in all of the elementary subjects. They are not all wrong. Many teachers use them intelligently as one avenue for teaching reading. But when instruction is reduced primarily to the basals, they violate "the primordial mode of being what we most essentially are."[11] More on this later.

What's Wrong with the Basals?

American teachers are beginning to articulate their sense that there is something deeply wrong about pressures on them to use basal instruction in ways that reduce learning to a measurable production function. One of the most forceful instances is the newspaper of Milwaukee teachers, *Rethinking Schools*. The newspaper was launched several years ago as a response to a variety of teacher discontent. Central among them was the school board's decision to implement an ambitious "curriculum and instruction management system" called Outcome Based Education.[12]

A prominent feature of this system is a reading instruction program at the grade-school level tied closely to a program of testing based on the basal readers. In *Rethinking Schools*, teachers report: "The basal reading program is so boring, fragmented, and workbook-oriented that many children learn to hate reading. . . . Few teachers can find the time to introduce whole books and more meaningful reading activities. . . . At the high school level . . . the competency test has turned the English Curriculum into a narrow rote program of drilling students for a test that does not measure what is really important for students to learn."[13]

To indicate that these criticisms are not unique, *Rethinking Schools* reported at length on the NCTE's *Report Card on Basal Readers.* To outline the emerging critique, here I list key ideas from the *Report Card* and supplement them with comments from Alan Luke's "Making 'Dick and Jane': Historical Genesis of the Modern Basal Reader." Regarding influence, the *Report Card* says that the use of basals is almost universal in American schools with far too many teachers following "the teacher's manual literally, seldom if ever exercising their own initiative and creativity in teaching reading."[14] "Dick and Jane" basals have become the twentieth-century archetype for a unified approach to the whole elementary curriculum with basal-type texts in science, social studies, arithmetic, health, and art.

In a scathing indictment of basal pedagogy the *Report Card* sketches several basic features:

- Reading is reduced to learning a word, a sound, or a skill at a time. Learning is sequential and skills are broken into components that can be controlled, explicitly taught, and then tested.
- The contrived language of texts is sequenced by a controlled vocabulary based on word lists leading to synthetic stories. There is more concern with controlling the sequence of sounds, words, and skills than in providing authentic language in the text.[15] Thus: "We can go. I can go. Can you go? Help! Help! I cannot go. I will help you. You can go. I *will* go."[16] (But why bother?)

Following in this vein, technical textbook writers transform traditional literature to fit their word lists. Here is Gerald McDermot's original rendition of a famous Japanese folktale:

Tasuko was a lowly stonecutter. Each day the sound of his hammer and chisel rang out as he chipped away at the foot of the mountain. He heaved the blocks of stone that formed the great temples and palaces.

He asked for nothing more than to work each day, and this pleased the spirit who lived in the mountains.

Harcourt's expert transformation of the beginning of this tale reads as follows:

Once there was a strong man. Each morning he went to the mountain. There he dug up stones. He broke them into pebbles with a large steel hammer. He carried them to the village where he sold them.[17]

With this as the fare, teachers are given an array of workbooks, skill sheets, and test materials designed to maintain children's "time on task."

As teachers are made accountable in terms of test scores, the school day is progressively narrowed to drill activities to produce "correct" answers to arbitrary test questions. (In the Holt Series, the NCTE found that 63 to 95 percent of the questions required only one correct answer.)[18] Having reduced the reality of reading to certain skill components, the measuring of these components is then treated as the reality of reading itself. The *Report Card* concludes: "So reading is not making sense of print anymore. It is doing well on the basal tests."[19]

Milwaukee teachers, gearing up to resist, found a quotation from Larry Cuban that described what was happening to them: "When the model curriculum standards are wired to the tests and texts, and then all are wired together to a larger accountability program (which means how you do on the tests is publicly disseminated), what you get is measurement-driven instruction, a rational bureaucratic systems management approach to teaching. . . . The creative and imaginative part of teaching shrinks."[20]

Genesis of the Basals

As John Dewey argued, a basic tool of understanding is to understand events in terms of the histories behind them. Therefore, a brief detour is in order here with the help of Allan Luke's "Making 'Dick and Jane': Historical Genesis of the Modern Basal Reader."[21]

We entered the twentieth century on the crest of the wave of industrialism and a progressive faith in science and technology as the engine of progress. The schools, confronting this reality and the challenge of burgeoning numbers of immigrant children, had to respond. National textbook companies that emerged in the opening decades found that the new educational psychology was ready to come to the rescue. As the McGuffey readers faded into history, mass production texts, with the imprimatur of science, were about to be created.

By World War II, the giants of educational psychology—Edward Thorndike, Arthur Gates, William Gray, and others—had created a new genre of school texts. Using scientific behaviorist theories of language development, graded texts were developed that were lexically, syntactically, and semantically controlled. They were augmented by workbooks, skill sheets, junior dictionaries, and administrator handbooks to provide expert supervision. After World War II, progressive refinements of "Dick and Jane" reading series pointed toward a thoroughgoing scientific orientation for curriculum development, pedagogical techniques, and assessment.

The systems approach to text making reflected a threefold rationale: the positivist conviction that all modern products and modes of human labor can be ordered on a linear scale of progress and development; the accompanying conviction that the teaching of reading can be envisioned as a matter of employing technically precise quantifiable programming of instruction that guarantees nearly universal success in literacy; and the belief that efficacy of teaching can be verified through the use of standardized tests. In the 1980s, a corollary was added: Teachers can be made accountable for scores and, in some cases, paid by results.[22]

Behind the whole project was the positivist faith in Thorndike's famous dictum: "Whatever exists, exists in some amount. To measure it is simply to know its varying amounts."[23] It is not surprising, then, to find that the logic of these convictions led in the 1980s to legislation in Texas which makes Texas teachers "subject to a $50 fine if they are caught teaching reading without an approved textbook" and to legislators in Florida passing a law making basal materials "the only legal means to provide reading instruction."[24]

As the movement gained momentum, the authors of *The Report Card on Basal Readers* saw that its logic centered more and more on the issue of control:

> More than anything else the basals are built around control: they control reading; they control language; they control learners; they control teachers. And this control becomes essential to the tight organization and sequence. Any relaxation of the control in any of these elements would appear to undermine the whole system. That's why publishers admonish teachers not to wander from the direction of the manuals; that's why administrators issue mandates requiring teachers to be faithful to the program.[25]

The Origins of Rational Control: Foucault

Some comments from Michel Foucault's *Discipline and Punish* throw light on the origins of this deep-seated need for rational control and explain why its taken-for-grantedness makes it so difficult to criticize. The great truth we must constantly hold before ourselves, said the French philosopher, is the realization that the rationality of the Enlightenment, which gave us the liberties, also invented the disciplines.[26]

Foucault was a critic of bureaucratic rationalization, which, in turn, is related to the positivist science tradition with roots in the Enlightenment. Foucault showed that, from the seventeenth and eighteenth centuries onward, there was a virtual takeoff in the increase of calculated power to control people in state apparatuses like the army, prisons, and tax administration. A vivid example is the transformation of the rowdy soldiers of the late middle ages into the eighteenth-century redcoats who could be converted into automatons by minute attention to detail in their training. As modern soldiers they were taught to remain motionless, never to look at the ground, and to move on command with bold, uniform steps, later to become the goose step. "Very good," Grand Duke Mikhail remarked to a regiment, after having kept it for an hour presenting arms, "only they breathe."[27]

We find the new controls also, says Foucault, in the fashioning of the late-seventeenth-century Christian Brothers schools for the poor. Jean Baptiste de la Salle, the founder, said: "How grave and dangerous is the task of teachers in the Christian Schools. . . . We must be concerned above all with the little things, the minute things in the lives of our students and their teachers. The little things lead to great results." Foucault adds: "The meticulousness of the regulations, the fussiness of inspections, the supervision of the smallest fragments of life and of the body will soon provide, in the context of the school, the barracks, the hospital, or the workplace, a technical rationality for the mystical calculus of the infinitesimal."[28]

Foucault noted that Jeremy Bentham's panopticon proposals for prisons and factories in the early 1800s embodied the technically inspired disciplines required for the modern era. (Panopticon comes from the Greek words *pan*, everything, and *opticon*, a place of sight—thus, a place to see everything.) Bentham elaborated panopticon plans for prisons, factories, and schools. The general idea included a basic circular building with cells for individual subjects around the inside of the circumference. In the center, facing the cells, is an inspector's tower with windows looking down on the cells. The observatory room at the top is constructed with a line of sight so that the inspector can see all while remaining invisible to the inmates below. Thus the basic principle was that "the persons to be inspected should always feel themselves as if under inspection."[29] The person to be supervised "is seen, but he does not see, he is the object of information, never a subject of communication."[30]

The guiding concept, says Foucault, is the ideal of the Perfect Gaze: the gaze that can see everything constantly. It employs three instruments for exercising power: hierarchical surveillance (all those intrusive gazes from the central office); normalizing judgment (aimed at securing conformity to the norm); and the examination. The gist of his argument is in his comments on the *examination* by which individuals may be measured, classified, and judged. In the examination, says Foucault, we can find a whole domain of knowledge and a whole type of power:

- Through techniques of the examination, individuals are made *visible*—subject to the gaze—and made into objects for measurement.
- By *documentation,* individuals and groups are encoded in written reports and files. They are organized into registers, classifications, and cumulative systems.
- By collecting documentary records on each individual, each is *individualized as a case* and becomes an object of knowledge and power connected with it.[31]

The examination is now pervasive in modern institutions. It is notably present, says Foucault, in the growth of larger, more systematized modern schools. The school has become, in fact, a sort of apparatus of uninterrupted examination, increasingly an arena for "a perpetual comparison of each and all that make it possible both to measure and judge."[32] My New York State informants tell me that a regent's student will take twenty-nine state-required examinations in twelve years. Only two years in the elementary school will be free of state-required exams.

The extension of the panopticon rationale throughout society coincided, Foucault says, with the rise of the human sciences. In line with the ideal of the Perfect Gaze, quantitative test scores and record keeping created the conditions for a technical matrix that changed discourse about policy issues into the neutral language of science. In schools, for example, talk about problems can be limited to the lexicon of technocratic ideology. Thus teachers are taught to think of classrooms as management systems and to discuss their teaching in terms of performance objectives, system components, sequencing of instruction, and the like. When the terminology of technical experts takes over, teachers may feel mute in the face of it: "Who are we to question scientific expertise?" If the system breaks down, the only answer of panopticon technicians is to do more of the same.

Gadamer on Humans as Dialogical Beings

If Foucault helps us see the sources of rational control, another European, German philosopher Hans-Georg Gadamer, might help us understand teachers' resistance. I want to report briefly here on two aspects of his work: his argument that positivist techniques threaten what is distinctive about us as human beings and his related ideas on the dialogical nature of language in achieving understanding. I am persuaded by Richard Bernstein's general argument in *Beyond Objectivism and Relativism* that Gadamer's whole effort was to see the nature of our being-in-the-world in a way that would be an alternative to the image of rational positivist science.[33] In *Truth and Method,* Gadamer holds that the right to converse—to hold a dialogue with texts and each other in reaching for understanding about the world and ourselves— is the distinctive characteristic of being human. For Gadamer understanding is more than epistemological. It is ontological in that we are "thrown into the world as beings constituted to understand and interpret: understanding is the original character of the being of human life itself."[34] Understanding underlies all human activity. And language is the medium in which we live. Therefore, the way we use it and learn it affects who we are and who we may become, and what our society is and what it can become.

    For Gadamer the chief task of hermeneutic philosophy

is to "correct the peculiar falsehood of modern consciousness"—that is, to defend practical reason against the domination of technology based on science and to oppose the
scientism of our age and the false idolatry of the expert that
pose a threat to practical and political reason.[35] From Gadamer's dialogical perspective, language is the means through
which we fulfill our essential task as *homo poeta:* to see the
world and ourselves with new meaning or understanding,
and with that understanding to transform the world and ourselves. To permit language teaching and learning to be
reduced to a series of skills that can be technically crafted
according to the rationale of behavioral science is to violate
something basic about ourselves.

It remains, then, to compare Gadamer's concept of the
dialogical role of language with the linear acquisition model
we saw in the basal readers. Although Gadamer does not treat
directly the topic of teaching reading, a glimpse at several
features of his discourse points to differences with the rationale of the basals: the quality of play in interpretive understanding; the role of prejudice in dialogue; and the ethical
dimension in the fusion of horizons for self-transformation
and world building.

Language as Interpretive Understanding

Gadamer wrote *Truth and Method* as his major effort to contrast the kind of truth available in interpretive understanding
with the kind of truth available in the positivist science tradition. Since the basals obviously are out of the Thorndike
positivist tradition, the juxtaposition of the basals versus Gadamer helps us see the differences that are at stake. In Gadamer's philosophical discourse, to understand implies the
possibility of seeing connections, of drawing conclusions, of
interpreting a "text, which may be a book, a work of art,
another person, or a life event."[36]

Gadamer notes that there is a similarity between playing games and reading a text. In each case there is a to-and-
fro movement: in a game, between the players and the game

Education, who is skeptical about the "time on task" obsession of instructional programs that leads early school learning to be so "cognitively anemic." In "The Value of 'Time Off Task': Young Children's Spontaneous Talk and Deliberate Text,"[45] she reported her observation of a teacher, motivated by the Russian psychologist Vygotsky, who attached value to providing "time off task"—informal peer talk to encourage higher-level intellectual work among primary-age children. Vygotsky held that intellectual reflection and imaginative world building can be consciously developed only after spontaneous conversation about such worlds.

This teacher broke out of the workbook frame. She viewed children's peer conversation as a natural outgrowth of their interest in each other and the work they were about. She encouraged children to converse as they created imaginary worlds with talk, pictures, and written texts. The children, who spoke different varieties of English and came from strikingly different home neighborhoods, entered the imaginative world of their classmates. Their lively interactions included challenges of logic, appreciation of vivid images, and sharing of feelings as they monitored and analyzed each other's stories. In time, a wide range of peer dialogue crept into texts, story boundaries were expanded, and complexity of plots emerged. Children were learning to listen to each other's words and to their own. In the process, they were engaging in what Gadamer calls *bildung*—self-transformation and the extension of world horizons.[46] As another teacher put it: "Little children do not need language broken up into drills and tests. Language and thought flourish in the rich imagery of children's invented worlds of fantasy and play and storytelling, of books and music and poetry. In such a climate children can fearlessly offer their hearts and minds to the meaning of language and the purpose of reading."[47]

Next, consider a couple of brief examples from *Rethinking Schools*. Teachers in a Madison, Wisconsin, elementary school reported their rejection of the belief that reading skills should be taught in fragments. They asked, "How many basal stories left an impact on you in your youth?" So they developed a "whole-book" approach that closely integrates reading, writing, and language arts—a program using real books by authors "who write with the purpose of communicating in some depth about the human condition."[48] Children engage in a variety of activities to enrich their understanding of an author's work: They blindfolded themselves when reading a story of a blind woman; they keep diaries as if they were one of the characters; they often correspond with the authors, including one from Holland who said his books had grown out of his experience as a war correspondent.

While convinced of the essential rightness of the whole-book method, the Madison teachers recognize that many teachers are used to basals and do not want to change. They hold that teachers should not be thrown into a whole-book approach, which takes time and collective effort, until they want to try it. At the same time they question the claim that teachers can easily "enrich" the basals. So many skills and lessons have to be covered, and the reading selections are so short that such activities are usually peripheral, even for the best-intentioned teachers, if not omitted altogether.

Finally, consider a report from *Rethinking Schools* about a rural school district in Pajaro Valley, California, with a heavy majority of Spanish-speaking farm and migrant workers.[49] To overcome the alienation of the children from their families, and to help parents increase their dignity and self-identity, a resort to dialogue between parents and children in reading and writing was developed. The children invited Spanish-speaking parents to a meeting with Alma Ada, a Mexican author, who talked with them about why and how she came to write stories for children's books.

Out of that effort has grown a program in which parents meet to discuss children's literature in Spanish and, more important, to read and discuss stories and poems written by their children—and by themselves. Their talk, following the work of Paulo Freire, includes description, critical analysis, and creative application to life situations. Videotapes record the parents reading the stories. The children watch their parents on the TV screen and join the discussion. Out of these readings, parents have come to spend time every evening with their children and with a book. They are taught at all times to encourage their children to reason and express themselves clearly, and to listen to the children with interest and affection. A book is now being compiled from the children's stories.

The Deeper Issue

In listening to the debate between advocates of the basals and their critics, we may hear it as simply a difference over teaching techniques. Gadamer's perspective reminds us, however, that the deeper issue is how children in a pluralist world will come to the use of language.

Of course, skill training (*techné*) is important, and that includes phonics, but the central role of language is as an instrument of understanding and practical/ethical judgment. Gadamer's concern is with "the peculiar falsehood of modern consciousness"—the domination of understanding and practical reason by technology based on science. When we turn schools into places of monologue where children are made to compete nervously for fragmented bits that score well on tests, we have perverted the educational enterprise before it starts. Those other teachers I described choose to bring their children to the use of language by making them members of dialogical communities. In doing so, they demonstrate what Gadamer has called "the noblest task—decision making according to one's own responsibility instead of conceding that task to others."[50] We need teachers who can experience themselves as architects of creative learning. And they need the conditions in their work to make that possible. In the chapters to follow, I will show that the bureaucratic bee-like controls which frustrate the creative work of teachers are also becoming dysfunctional in the workplaces of Americans across the board.

Three

Americans at Work: Architects or Bees?

While the denigrating treatment of teachers and students was increasing in the 1980s, some very different developments were appearing in industry. The fragmented, control-centered management style that was being brought into the schools to improve performance was being challenged in key segments of industry as the very source of productivity problems.

In 1980, a luncheon meeting comment by William Duffy, vice-president of General Motors in charge of new plant design, helped me get the point. "GM used to boast," he said, "that the production line had been broken down into segments so small that any production task could be taught in fifteen minutes or less; any idiot could learn it. If workmanship and morale were poor, the answer was to step up supervision and control. GM is now concerned," he said, "that a model based on increased control by supervisors of a bored, reluctant work force which produces shabby products is not viable for survival."

In the face of the Japanese achievement of producing cars of superior quality produced by combining creative technology with the collaborative efforts of a committed work force, GM felt it had to pursue its own version of a similar course. By 1990, GM was ready to launch Saturn, "the car of the future," by combining high-tech robotics and a new style of work relations. Agreements were worked out with the United Auto Workers to change the status of assembly-line workers from hourly laborers to salaried employees. Union workers are to be involved in decision making that formerly was the sole prerogative of management. Workers in production teams of six to fifteen people have responsibilities for workplace decisions and quality control. This work style is combined with "computer-integrated manufacturing." (More on this later.)

Changes in Work

To see what lay behind this transformation we may note the transition in production style that has taken place in American society—from our rural beginning, through the creation of the assembly line in the early 1900s, to a work style emerging under high tech as the century closes. We are now at the beginning of a third major change in American work life. At our beginning, in the late 1700s, we had broken with feudal restrictions and inequalities and were overwhelmingly self-employed (other than the shame of slavery)—in farming, the trades, and small commercial enterprises. Some 80 percent of nonslave Americans worked on farms; by 1900 that portion had been halved to 41 percent and by 1990 to 3 percent.[1]

As we entered the twentieth century, the corporate industrial revolution was creating a radically different work world. In this second stage, pyramidal corporate bureaucracies with top-down managerial directives became the American way of work. The great majority of Americans hired out their labor to organizations. Democracy was held to belong in the political realm with its periodic opportunities to vote. In daily work life, it was argued that democratic processes were irrelevant because competitive reality decreed acceptance of "command and control" managerial authority—the prerogatives of management.

The design of industrial-era work remained largely within the parameters established by its founder, Frederick W. Taylor. Thinking, planning, and detailed job design were reserved for the administrator-engineer technical planners at the top. Execution of prescribed, detailed tasks under supervised control was the job for those lower down.

We are now in the beginning of stage three: the electronic/computer revolution accompanied by the emergence of a global competitive market and dangerous ecological damage due to expanding populations and industrial growth. Under the lash of the computer revolution and the competitive world economy, unprecedented changes are under way. The much heralded shift from smokestack industries to the service sector, for example, is already far advanced. In 1985, only 19 percent of workers were employed in manufacturing, while information workers alone—clerks, sales, technical, professional, and managerial people—made up 53 percent of the labor force.[2] In 1970 there were only about 200 robots in all American factories. But between 1970 and 1980 General Motors' wage bill soared by 240 percent, while the cost of a robot had stabilized at $5 to $6 per hour. The result: 5,000 robots in GM plants by 1985 with an estimated 15,000 by 1990.[3]

Even while the labor force is being reduced in manufacturing there are serious shortages of workers equipped to handle the complexities of computer-aided manufacturing. A recent report noted that manufacturing is increasingly about working with high-tech equipment. In plants where the Stealth plane is produced, workers are required to drive fasteners with tolerances as close as a thousandth of an inch into contoured surfaces designed to elude radar. Machinists operate computerized tool-making devices. Other workers mold composite materials like graphite to make fighter fuselages.

In California some aerospace firms, worried about the shortage of skilled, motivated workers, have linked themselves to community colleges to offer degree programs to workers in manufacturing technology with training in manufacturing, materials, drafting, machinery, and computer-aided design. The goal is to secure multiple-skilled, flexible employees. Salaries are in the $40,000 to $50,000 range.[4]

In the nuclear industry, highly educated, highly motivated workers are essential. A consultant for teamwork at Three Mile Island said, "We're moving increasingly into dangerous, unforgiving technologies that can't be operated safely with uncommitted people."[5]

About half of Americans now work in offices. A Stanford study pointed out that although office automation created new jobs for skilled clerical workers, it eliminated thousands of jobs for low-skilled clerical workers and many professional jobs in the middle of the career ladder. The insurance industry is an example where the bottom and middle levels of the work force are shrinking.[6]

As a number of observers have pointed out, the real world of work is much more complex than a solid rush to computer-dominated labor. The Bureau of Labor Standards did project for the 1978–1990 period an increase of more than 100 percent for computer operators, system analysts, and machine mechanics—high-tech jobs. But focusing on the *rate* of change alone can distort matters. The number of *actual* job increases is quite different. The five occupations projected to produce the most jobs were all in low-skilled areas: janitors, nurse's aides, sales clerks, cashiers, and food workers.[7] Beyond that, of course, is the steady drift toward a dual economy: the new billionaires at the top, many affluent Americans in high-tech and professional jobs, and a growing underclass, often people of color, in a quasi-permanent condition of unemployment and poverty. Some 20 percent or more of American children are growing up in families below the poverty level.

What are we to make of such dramatic changes? Will high-tech production raise the skill level of work, or will it extend the spread of deskilling? Will it create more jobs than are eliminated? What jobs will be eliminated, what jobs created? We are too caught in the middle of the revolution to understand it fully. Who could have predicted the ramifications for American life when Henry Ford got the gleam in his eye for a mass-produced horseless carriage?

One may find examples of both deskilling and upgrading of skills. Deskilling does go on. Every time we enter a fast-food restaurant we see deskilling at work. In apparel factories, automatic machines can now perform certain tasks like pocket setting that permit the hiring of machine tenders to replace skilled workers. By the opening of the 1990s, however, evidence is mounting to support the opposite trend: the upgrading of skills. Thomas Bailey, research scholar at the Conservation of Human Resources Project at Columbia University, reported on a series of in-depth studies of four different industries: apparel, textiles, banking, and business services.[8] In these industries, it was clear that new technology could be designed to either deskill or upskill work, but the trend is in the latter direction. The reason is that increased international competition, changes in both industrial structure and consumer demand, and the capacity of technology to help meet these challenges act as forces to push skill levels upward.

Because of the intensity of international competition, U.S. companies in these industries are under growing pressure to be more responsive to divergent consumer demands, to lower costs, to reduce defective goods, and to cut levels of inventories. Each of the four industries has been making adjustments. Traditional production once centered on providing a few standardized goods or services; companies now offer dozens of customized products.

Banks, for example, instead of offering just savings and checking accounts, now merchandise dozens of products, including certificates of deposit, IRAs, money market funds, and brokerage accounts. Low-skilled jobs are being phased out. Automatic teller machines and computer systems lead to replacement of tellers and clerk typists who could function with a high school education. Messengers who carried applications typed by clerk typists from station to station are being replaced by the computer communications system. Meanwhile, "platform personnel" now perform myriad tasks with customers interested in the wide array of new products. They often have postsecondary education.

Until very recently, the apparel and textile industries were trying to stay competitive by an automating strategy. The tactic was to maximize the output of operators by isolating and then automating each stage of the production process. This tactic eliminated many low-skill operations. It was an effective way to produce large quantities of mass-produced goods for the huge American market. The industry faced a radically different situation, however, when the customers became international and a strong demand for a variety of products took off. The apparel industry used to plan in terms of two fashion seasons. Now designers may change their lines six times a year, and retailers clamor for continuous changes in their stock. If firms stayed with the old industrial style, orders for new products could not be filled and large inventories of unwanted, unsold products accumulated at season's end.

One response to the need for a quick turnaround on a variety of products has been a new interest in "modular manufacturing." Garment shops traditionally were organized around functional departments—all buttonhole operators and their machines were in one department, pocket setters in another, and so forth, with separate supervisors for each. The different functions had to be linearly coordinated, one following another. In the modular approach, groups of operators and their machines are placed in a circle configuration and work together to assemble an entire garment. After an operator completes one task, the garment goes on to the next operator. Hence products can be modified for customers with different needs. Many of the actual sewing tasks remain the same, but the modular system fundamentally changes the nature of the job. Workers have to coordinate their efforts. If one operator is falling behind, another group member can be there to help. If someone does defective work, it will be noticed by the next worker in the circle. Bottlenecks are corrected by group action, often without the intervention of a supervisor.

Tasks of other workers ancillary to the group are also affected. Supervisors must now have a full understanding of the whole product. They must know how to meet the needs of customers and have ongoing relations with suppliers. These matters used to be handled by central management. But computers can now diffuse the information throughout the company and supervisors in coordination with the group teams make the adjustments required. Maintenance personnel who used to repair a few machines must now repair many. They must expect to face new types of machines in the future, and many of the new ones will have microprocessors and other electronic components. Traditional skills are no longer adequate. Mechanics must be students of the processes transforming the machines for which they are responsible. Sue Berryman of the Institute on Education and the Economy, Columbia University, notes: "To understand, diagnose, and fix the new machines, technicians have to be able to represent the structures and processes of these machines *symbolically* in their heads. To do this they have to be able to follow complicated manuals, diagrams, and updates provided by manufacturers. Literacy requirements accordingly shot up."[9]

What comes through in all these industries is an image of a work environment in constant change due to new technology, new products, and new trade patterns. To cope, firms need employees capable of working in more fluid nonroutine environments. Recognizing this, companies experiencing fast technological change have tended to employ workers with higher levels of education. Better-educated workers seem to be the ones who have more flexibility and the capacity for further learning. Successful textile and apparel firms increasingly are sending their workers to local community colleges for upgrading, and that pattern is being followed by progressive companies in other industries. In summary, all four of these industries are being forced to respond to similar pressures: the impact of microelectronics, the intensification of competition, changes in customer demand, and the pace of accelerated technological and market changes.

Some caution about generalizing from this study is in order because these companies tend to be the more forward-looking types. To the extent that they do represent a trend, however, the picture emerging is clear. The effect of modern technology and organizational change is to increase the demand for better-educated employees, to make middle-level jobs more demanding, and to continue to eliminate or reduce low-skilled jobs. A key need will be for managers who know how to make the best use of human resources. Workers without the skills and education to adapt to this evolving economy face a constrained and grim future.

The one thing we can be sure of is that we are confronted with turbulent change: change that is rapid and unpredictable. Robert Reich in *The Next American Frontier* argues that to be confidently competitive in the global market we need a formula to bring together inventive technology with flexible, intelligent response by a committed, engaged work force.[10] Our vulnerability in the world market has been due, to some extent, to the failure of traditional management to produce such results. As this failure grows more pronounced, it becomes evident that a new theory of work design is essential. A leading alternative is democratic sociotechnical work theory.

Democratic Sociotechnical Design for Work

Clarifying this new philosophy of work has been an international process conducted by American thinkers like Erich Trist and Michael Maccoby, Norwegians like Einar Thorsrud and P. G. Herbst, and the Australian Fred Emery.[11] As evidence of trouble at work accumulated in the 1970s—shabby quality, absenteeism, apathy, drug and alcohol abuse—one response was mounted by sociotechnical theorists who attacked the Taylorist tradition of scientific management. As noted in Chapter One, they found Taylorism guilty of the "technical fix" error: the assumption that all problems will yield to expert-designed technical solutions. The reality of human work, these critics said, is "socio" as well as "technical." "Socio" refers to the communicative, collaborative, idea-generating aspects of human beings. The mainstream efficiency model is out of touch with the "socio" dimension. It falters because it fails to engage the commitment and personal enthusiasm of people, as well as their capacity for learning and problem solving. The new theorists held that the old production model is fundamentally out of touch with the turbulent change of postindustrial reality.

The capacity to cope successfully with change depends on building a learning capacity into the system itself. As we have seen, there is an undeniable trend in the direction of "horizontal-participative" management by leading corporations that are succeeding best in the third stage. Plants designed with the most innovative sociotechnical methods report that these units are 30 to 50 percent more productive than their counterparts. Richard Walton of the Harvard Business School says that advanced computer technology calls for a radical change in traditional work practices. The traditional method of dividing work into discrete low-skill tasks becomes obsolete in the computer-integrated workplace where many functions—including materials handling, assembly, inventory control, and testing—are integrated by computer. As *Business Week* noted: "The integration no longer makes it possible to define jobs individually or measure individuals' performance. . . . It requires a collection of people to manage a segment of technology and perform as a team."[12]

Dramatic evidence of change has occurred in one of America's most beleaguered, conflict-ridden industries: automobile manufacturing.[13] The changes have come gradually and with pain—motivated by a dramatic loss of market to the Japanese and other foreign competitors with losses of billions of dollars in the late 1970s and 1980s. Management reluctantly concluded that it must change to survive.

The auto industry had always been the epitome of Taylorized production with workers viewed as extensions of machinery—treated as nonpersons by a top-down management style. One response in the 1930s was the creation of the militant United Auto Workers, which came into being with pitched battles against Pinkerton strikebreakers and classic auto plant sit-ins. Union/management negotiations were confrontational—marked by bitterness and suspicion.

When management, gradually in the 1980s, decided it must give workers more say about their jobs and life in the plants, many workers viewed the moves with deep distrust. Quality-of-work-life (QWL) proposals that led to improved efficiency were seen as ploys by management to reduce the work force or to squeeze out more work. Management claimed American workers were lazy, sloppy, irresponsible.

As the Japanese inroads continued in the 1980s, leaders in both management and the unions began to see the necessity for change. This need was underscored when American workers under Japanese collaborative management produced fine-car quality. A dramatic example was the joint GM/Toyota plant in Fremont, California. It had been closed in 1982 because it assembled cars of poor quality and labor relations bordered on anarchy—with 20 percent absenteeism on a normal day. Changes in management style were introduced: Workers were organized into teams and given a voice in making changes in the assembly process; status symbols such as reserved parking for managers and executive dining rooms were eliminated; union/management consultation was introduced on issues like layoffs, changes in production schedules, and day-to-day work decisions. The changes demonstrated that with proper training and motivation an American work force—even one with a terrible record—could produce high-quality cars economically.

As the decade unfolded, the major auto companies started consultative procedures on health and safety issues and ergonomic studies to create job conditions that would improve workers' performance and their well-being. These approaches led to visible results that built confidence. Ford introduced employee involvement practices. At the Romeo, Michigan, plant workers are organized into groups where they learn all of the jobs performed by their team. This strategy reduces boredom and allows for a more flexible manufacturing process. Workers are trained eight to twelve weeks before they are given a permanent team assignment. To break down distrust, workers are given a great deal of information about the plant and its performance. Moreover, a computerized communication system allows a worker to ask a question of any manager in the plant—and get an answer.

As the American version of employee involvement is emerging, in some cases workers are being given a greater role in the plant and the company than the Japanese model permits. At GM's Saturn plant, for example, workers are given a voice in the selection of suppliers, dealers, and advertising agencies. Work teams are listened to seriously for their ideas on how to improve quality and cut costs. At the UAW's national economic convention in 1990, union president Owen Bieber demanded a greater role for workers at every level when contracts are being negotiated. He called for an end to management's "charmed circle of privilege," saying that the industry's survival depends on workers' involvement in deciding investments, products, prices, and working conditions. He insisted that management cut its own ranks and reduce its salaries before even thinking about laying off workers. He charged management with an obsession with short-term profits at the expense of long-term planning and demanded that workers should be involved in decisions to send work overseas. It was time, he said, to let fully motivated, fully secure workers contribute to corporate success.

It is not all going smoothly. Some plants do better in the transition than others. One of the big obstacles to the team concept can be management. Team leaders replace foremen and function as problem solvers who encourage, counsel, and provide resources rather than being mere spear-carriers for management. The result is a thinning out of layers of middle management. Not only the traditional role of management is being challenged but the jobs themselves. Fierce debates go on in the unions, too. Those who advocate the new style, like Owen Bieber, UAW president, are sometimes accused of jumping into bed with management, and team-style work can be upsetting to workers who find security in following job specifications guaranteed in the contract. Puzzling new questions arise: If profits go up, what procedure determines how they should be shared?

As America entered the 1990s, despite anxiety about change and occasional failures and resistance, the trend toward new work continued in small companies as well as in big corporations. There is, for example, a 1990 report by Ralph Stayer, chief executive of Johnsonville Foods, a family-owned sausage plant in Sheboygan, Wisconsin, who describes changes introduced when the company was in trouble in 1980.[14] He took the risk of putting his workers in charge—the same people who had been bored and made careless costly errors now run the company. They buy equipment, write budgets, hire and fire. Sales have increased 20 percent annually since the changes were made, and productivity has increased 50 percent since 1986.

Among major corporations the trend continues to grow. A survey of 476 Fortune 1000 companies found that 46 percent had some employees in self-managed work teams, compared with 27 percent three years previously. Features of a new work style show up in companies across the board. There are work teams without bosses who set profit goals, write schedules, develop products, meet customers, design assembly lines, and pore over financial records. At a General Mills plant in Georgia, workers do their own maintenance, scheduling, and clerical jobs, make quality checks, handle disciplinary problems, and participate in the interviewing and hiring of new employees.

A Goodyear plant in Iowa has no seniority, no time clock, no suspensions—just a manager and teams with rotating coordinators. "It's nothing like a factory," one worker said. "You're actually in on everything—from making it to sending it out the door. It's not the same old grind every day. You don't get burned out. You're actually making your own decisions, using your own judgment."[15]

Achieving true employee involvement is a slow and difficult process, but once respect for the dignity and intelligence of workers is built into the process, there probably is no turning back. Shoshanna Zuboff's *In the Age of the Smart Machine* offers a deeper perception of what is at stake in these changes. Zuboff, professor of organizational behavior at Harvard's Business School, explored the issues by studying what is happening in work settings where high tech is in its advanced stage.[16] (Here we note simply that main features of her argument. We will return later to examples from industry.)

The thrust of her argument is that we have accumulated enough experience with powerful new computer technologies to see that they confront us with two very different possibilities of what can happen to both the quality of production and the worker's quality of life. Work can be designed to increase centralized command control while reducing humans to deskilled, programmed functionaries; or it can be designed to produce dramatically different results. To sketch the differences, Zuboff projects for us two scenarios. As she describes it, the choices we face concern the conception and distribution of knowledge and power in the workplace.

Scenario I involves computer-mediated work: the "automated" option. It is one where computer technology is designed essentially as a nineteenth-century machine system—with technology performing processes formerly done by human hands, only with more continuity and control. Intelligence is located in the "smart machine," replacing critical judgments of the work force. Retaining exclusive control of the organization's knowledge base, managers use the new technology to structure the organization to preserve their prerogatives of command and the hierarchical distance that sets them apart from subordinates. They may use the new technology to create new forms of surveillance and new techniques of remote, automated management that enhance centralized control. This scenario moves in that direction of rational control so vividly described by Foucault. In response, workers may invent new methods of protection and escape—becoming dependent, resentful, apathetic, resorting to drugs, or adversarial conflict.

Scenario II, the "informated" option, projects a very different possibility. Here the new computer technology becomes a source for designing innovative methods of sharing information through social communication and reflection. Organizational leaders recognize that new skills and new knowledge are needed by the work force to tap the potential of intelligent technology—a technology that produces a more abstract kind of work that depends on understanding and manipulation of information. The new work milieu requires innovative methods of information sharing and social exchange. Work relations become more collaborative and bound by intricate relationships. As a new array of work tasks emerges out of the data-rich environment, jobs are imbued with more challenge and meaning. Hierarchical distinctions begin to blur as the new technology integrates information across time and space. Managers and workers fashion new roles that permit creative responses, as well as opportunities to add value to products and services. "These methods in turn," says Zuboff, "produce a deepened sense of responsibility and joint ownership, as access to ever broader domains of information lends new objectivity to data and preempts the dictates of hierarchical authority."[17]

Work trend projections leave no doubt that low-skilled, automated production can be used to control American workers. Or, alternatively, work may be sent overseas—"offshored"—where wages are dramatically lower. Scenario I's use of technology is already being transferred to the Asian Rim and elsewhere.

But Scenario II, which combines inventive technology with a well-educated, engaged work force capable of learning, is what our long-term welfare depends on. These developments are forcing corporate leaders to consider what learning styles are required for the new conditions. They are convinced that a viable work force depends on having employees who have strong number and literacy skills—and above all the ability to learn, to think abstractly and contextually, and to collaborate in problem solving. Yet grave doubts have arisen as to whether we can design an education capable of producing the communication skills and conceptual thinking ability required by a change-driven work environment.

When these doubts arise, there is a tendency to turn an envious look toward the Japanese. After all, they seem to have pulled together an educational approach combined with a work style that is awesomely effective for the challenges of our time. The question is whether we can find the answer to our problems by looking to a model that seems to work so well for the Japanese.

═══ *Four* ═══

The Japanese Model: Can It Work for Us?

In 1986, I reviewed a book by Benjamin Duke, *The Japanese School: Lessons for Industrial America*—a book that is unusually perceptive about the nature of the Japanese system. I believe it has lessons for us beyond those mentioned by Duke. Certainly Duke has the right credentials for his task. Not only has he taught in the public schools in the United States, but for the past twenty-five years he has been professor of comparative and international education at the International Christian University in Tokyo.

Are we a nation at risk? Duke answers with a qualified no; but he argues that we are under real and increasingly severe challenge in the world market. We can gain insight into our difficulties if we try to understand the sources of the Japanese economic miracle. We miss the point, he says, by rushing directly to the Japanese factories or the Ministry of Trade and Industry to learn about Japan's competitive effectiveness. The source of the challenge to industrial America, Duke argues, lies in Japanese traditions and values and in the role of the school in transmitting those values: "It is the

Japanese school that functions as one of the major, if not the most critical, instruments within the infrastructure of Japanese society, carefully and painstakingly nurturing and perpetuating the basic qualities of the Japanese worker."[1]

Three features of the Japanese school system stand out in Duke's account: a fierce competitive examination system centered on basic skill instruction; a motivational attitude of *"gambare,"* which roughly translates into "never give up"; and loyalty to the group and the Japanese style of group leadership. Certainly the system has produced staggeringly effective results. Over 90 percent of the students graduate from high school with among the highest standardized test scores in the world—compared with 75 percent high school completion in the United States (with more than 40 percent dropping out in our chief metropolis, New York City) and an estimated 23 million functional illiterates.

Duke warns against the temptation of Americans to reach out primarily for the Japanese school features they most readily understand: a uniform, expert-designed curriculum combined with exam-driven instruction. Such thinking fits our present illusion that we can find a quick fix to restore American preeminence by imbuing our children with rugged individualism—the goal of being Number One above all else and driving teachers into action by the lash of accountability. It is self-delusion to assume that such a simple formula is at the heart of the Japanese accomplishment.

The strength of Duke's analysis lies in his insistence on the intrinsic interdependence of Japanese school life with the total cultural experience. To grasp the nature of the Japanese system and its style we must understand its origins in the Japanese view of their historical condition as a vulnerable, embattled people and in the persistent influence of the spiritual tradition of Bushido.

History and Bushido

From their earliest years in school, Japanese children are made aware of their country's critical geographical limitations. Because of the predominance of mountainous, forested terrain, Japan has the equivalent of half of the U.S. population living in an area smaller than Montana. The children learn that the nation is incapable of feeding itself and must import 85 percent of its energy. They learn of the heroic sacrifices of their ancestors who repeatedly faced the natural disasters of earthquakes, typhoons, volcanic eruptions, and massive floodings—phenomena that remain contemporary dangers.

Coming out of World War II as a defeated nation with its industrial infrastructure in disarray, Japan faced the future with a heightened sense of its vulnerability. To avoid starvation and bitter poverty it had to be successful in industrial production and international trade. With a clear sense of the urgency of moving into a technological industrial reality with no time to lose, a national consensus emerged to create what they saw as the American model: a mass educational system through high school that would produce a literate, mathematically competent work force—but a work force imbued with a distinctive Japanese work commitment. Since survival itself was at stake, the creation of such a mass school system to produce competent, diligent, loyal workers won unquestioned national support.

Japanese students also learn that as citizens of one of the most racially unified nations of the world they share an ancient tradition and a common set of values that has been a perennial source of strength. The centerpiece is the ethical code of Bushido. Inazo Nitobe, the great interpreter of Japanese culture to the West at the opening of the twentieth century, stated that unless one understands feudalism and Bushido, the moral ideas of modern Japan are incomprehensible. We can only hint here at its essence and refer the reader to Nitobe's own account, "Bushido as an Ethical System."[2]

Bu-shi-do, literally the Military Knight Ways, is the moral code of the feudal samurai warriors. At its heart is loyalty to one's lord and clan. Related to loyalty is a cluster of virtues: duty (to parents, superiors, inferiors, and the nation); integrity and justice; courage and unflinching forti-

tude; correct manners and strict observance of propriety; maintenance of honor and shunning of shame; and self-control
illustrated in endurance of pain, indifference to death, and
disdain of worldly wealth. Bushido, which began as the code
of the elite, spread over time until it provided the moral standards for the whole people.

Nitobe explains how Bushido penetrated Japanese
character since it was supported by the main spiritual traditions of the islands: Buddhism furnished a sense of trust in
fate, stoic composure in the face of disaster, and a quality of
putting oneself in harmony with the absolute; Shintoism centered on loyalty to the emperor, faithfulness to the people of
the island nation, and reverence for ancestral memory and
filial piety; Confucianism stressed the doctrine of right order
or harmony under heaven, the quality of moral obligation to
the family, and the bonds and duties obtaining between the
governing and the governed. Within the Bushido tradition,
the value of *gambare* plays a key role in the fierce committed
Japanese effort at work or school. Duke maintains that the
commitment to *gambare* (persistent all-out effort) characterizes
Japanese society to its roots. The ordinary Japanese lives with
a deep sense of conscientiousness in carrying out responsibility to the group: "He is forever encouraged by his leader or,
in the case of students, his teacher, as well as by his fellow
workers or students, to *gambare.* This serves as a constant
reminder that every member of the group or the *kumi* (classroom) rides in the same narrow ship perpetually sailing along-
side a precipice. All must *gambare* together to avoid
catastrophe, to avoid going over the edge."[3]

The Japanese classroom embraces this traditional code
of values and demonstrates why the Japanese worker is often
characterized as loyal, diligent, competent, and competitive.
In fact, Duke says that "a visit to the public elementary school
located several blocks away from a factory will provide far
deeper insights into the Japanese miracle than will a visit to
the plant site itself. . . . The challenge to industrial America
from Japan lies primarily in the Japanese classroom rather
than the factory."[4] Duke offers three chapters to make his

argument: "The Loyal Worker—Kumi: The Group"; "The Literate Worker—Kokugo: The National Language"; and "The Competent Worker—Sugaku: Mathematics."

The first-grade classroom, the *kumi*, wastes no time in teaching "the very stuff of being Japanese"—loyalty to the group to achieve group harmony. The new first-grader is assigned to a *kumi* of forty to forty-five students with whom he will be in close contact for two school years of 230 days each (compared to 180 in the United States). Sitting in straight rows in regular seats, *kumi* members study uniform lessons, play together as a unit on the playground, eat together in classroom seats, and do janitorial duties. The teacher assiduously aims to cultivate pride in the *kumi*, telling students that the *kumi* depends on each of them—on their *gambare* and on their duty never to let the group down.

The teacher teaches the *kumi* as a single unit moving at a single pace. In reading, for example, all forty-five students use the same book and are taught the same lesson at the same time, often reading in chorus. In writing or drawing, all write the same characters or draw the same objects (which, in all their similarity, are proudly posted on the walls). Uniform group routine is the method for teaching competency in skills as prescribed in the teacher's handbook. The teacher assumes the obligation of assuring mastery by each student. This rote discipline is supplemented, however, by teaching the traditional skills of Japanese group membership. The class is divided into small groups known as *han*, each led by an elected *han-cho*. The *han* take on various duties such as preparing a group report on a science project or field trip, serving lunch to the class from the central kitchen, cleaning the room, mopping the halls, cleaning the toilets.

In the *han*, children learn the group decision-making skills that later will be employed in quality control circles. The *han-cho* must learn the subtleties of Japanese leadership, which are passed along by the teacher and reinforced at home. *Han-cho* must learn to lead without leading too much, for humility is valued. They must listen carefully to all opinions in the group. Their responsibility is to harmonize the group attitude by reconciling various positions and moving to consensus. Fairness must prevail so that members feel they are part of the decision-making process through mutual understanding. It is the essence of Japanese-style democracy—in the classroom, on the shop floor, in executive offices.

Its roots go back to the precepts of Prince Shotoku Taishi in his constitution of A.D. 604. Harmony can be achieved, he held, when decisions on important matters are not made by one person alone but discussed by many so as to arrive at a right decision in concert with others. Thus when the Japanese studied new American management theory in the 1950s by theorists like Maslow, McGregor, Herzberg, Likert, and Argyris it seemed to confirm their tradition of group process, and so they introduced industrial-quality control circles. It was a style of management that made no significant headway in U.S. industry until the 1980s, and then only in a segment of American management.

The emerging Japanese consensus favored a school system that would give equal weight to group process and academic competence. The entire population assumed that every young person entering the work force had to be capable of reading instructions on the operation and care of new machines and technology and had to have the mathematical skill and comprehension to function in a technological workplace. While the method reduces to a numbing step-by-step group instruction following the national teacher's guide— memorize, repeat, drill, and test—teachers can count on strong family and societal support. There are, for example, enormous pressures on the child by the family to read, write, and figure, especially through the *kyoiku mama*, the educationally minded mother. After an 8:30–3:30 schoolday, children are expected to devote hours of study at home, memorizing and taking mock exams. For many there is supplementary exam preparation in after-school *juku* classes or Saturday afternoon and Sunday *yobiku* classes, and instructional programs are regularly shown on TV. These special after-school cram classes point to the extra crutch every Japanese teacher can rely on: the notorious high school and university admission examinations, referred to by critics as "Exam Hells."

The instructional effort in mathematics is given support by a national lobby whose main purpose is to maintain high standards in math. While teachers in general are highly respected, this is especially true for mathematics teachers. Their salaries are competitive with those in industry. A beginning math teacher in Tokyo starts at $737 per month, compared to a new engineer at Hitachi at $762.

The most striking lesson from Duke's look at Japanese schools is how profoundly different the two societies are from each other. There is, for example, nothing in the Japanese experience of the feeling of the open frontier and boundless natural resources or the diversity of race, ethnicity, and language. The spiritual heritages are dissimilar, as well, so that the competitive spirit that both seem to share turns out to be very different on closer look. It is a distorted caricature to equate Japanese *gambare* with American individualistic competitiveness.

Nevertheless, Duke maintains that the two societies can learn from each other. The Japanese have unquestioned strength, he says, in *instruction* of the basics; but they are weak in education. They lack the strengths of the Dewey tradition with its emphasis on the cultivation of inquiry, individuality, and creativity. Japanese critics of the Exam Hell are arguing that Japan will be handicapped in meeting the challenge of change in the twenty-first century if it keeps the present system. Frustration comes, however, from the Japanese desire to cultivate creativity while retaining the goal of a competent, loyal work force produced by the "examination fix." Exam-driven instruction is the tar baby to which they are stuck.

Facing the Societal Facts

Duke's analysis of the school/culture linkages in Japan is masterful. I have concentrated on it here because it is the strength of his book. When, however, he turns to "lessons for the United States," he concentrates on *school* recommendations and fails to seriously address the societal context. He sees the American school system as having a glaring two-tier quality that is a source of both its strengths and weaknesses.

We are not "at risk," he thinks, because the best schools in our two-tiered system are unquestionably excellent from any comparative perspective. Their graduates lead the world in technological advances, evidenced by Americans winning half of all the Nobel Prizes since World War II and writing 38 percent of the world's scientific and technical articles in recent years. "As long as our good schools produce the kinds of graduates they do today," concludes Duke, "we would be wise not to tamper too much with them."[5]

The trouble point, he says, is with the education of the average and below-average student in the basics from the first grade onward. He gives a dramatic picture of the educational inequalities in the two-tiered system when he reports on his visits to one of the best suburban schools and an inner-city high school thirty minutes away. He notes the striking differences in the physical plant: the library facilities, resource centers, lounges, classrooms, and lavatories. He notes the armed guards that greeted him in the inner-city school and the feeling of potential violence in the school and the community surrounding it.

While he deplores these enormous discrepancies and holds that we will become increasingly vulnerable with millions of dysfunctional semiliterate workers, his final recommendations boil down to two suggestions for school changes: Make a national commitment to see that every student attains the literary and numerary proficiency to meet the requirements of high-tech workplaces (although he does not think we need to copy the Japanese Exam Hell), and instill the attitude of *gambare* into American students, teachers, and administrators with the warning that our standard of living is at stake. (We should relinquish the idea that more money alone will save us.)

He simply never gets around to the blunt fact that without a firm commitment to remove the social cancer of ghetto poverty, injustice, and violence, the calls for greater skill competency and *gambare* are empty rhetoric. We can only guess what might follow from his recommendations if ghetto youth had access to what Duke says are the postgraduation expectations of the average Japanese high school student. He says the Japanese get alarmed when unemployment reaches 2.6 percent, compared to 40 percent in some American inner-city areas. Suppose American minority youth were leaving school with near certainty of a job with a company committed to providing lifelong employment—a company where, in slack times, managers take the first cut in pay and make great efforts to avoid layoffs; a company where workers' ideas on how to improve the quality of product and work life are listened to seriously; a company in which there is a constant upgrading of technical and communication skills and rotations of work roles.

We should not fool ourselves. If American ghetto life remains unchanged, we choose not only to have a crippled work force but a bill of $20,000 per year per prison inmate for the incarceration of tens of thousands. Japan enters world competition with no comparable economic or moral handicap.

Finally, Duke says, Japanese society has functioned effectively primarily because of the voluntary commitment of individuals to the welfare of groups. The Japanese attain social effectiveness in work and schooling by combining technical efficiency with the values of group loyalty and effort of their own Bushido philosophy. We cannot help but admire their efforts. Their model helps us see the shortsightedness of campaigns to win the day by technical efficiency alone. When *yang* is not balanced by *yin*, there is disorder under heaven. We know the Bushido philosophy cannot be transplanted to our shores. But in the chapters to follow we explore American efforts to energize ourselves by combining the power of electronic technology with values from our own traditions.

Five

The Choice We Face:
Automate or Informate?

America may feel the lure of the Japanese model. We could always use more *gambare* (persistent all-out effort), of course, and we might like the idea of getting a quick fix by mimicking the Japanese. But we delude ourselves if we think we can get it by copying some external trappings: group competition, rote methods, and the motivation of Exam Hells. All of these practices get their unique power from the heritage of the samurai warriors (their Bushido ethics) and an island people's awareness of their vulnerability.

We do well to note Benjamin Duke's final reminder that the effectiveness of Japanese society derives primarily from one source: the voluntary commitment of individuals to the welfare of groups. We need that same source of strength. Rather than assuming that we can find our way by copying the Japanese, we need to find strength in our own cultural roots—that is, from the values of our democratic tradition that will help us create our own distinctive American style for meeting the challenge of electronic-era realities. It will not be easy, however, in either industry or schooling, for the

53

need to incorporate democratic values is in tension with both the command-control traditions of corporate bureaucracies as well as the rugged individualism that accompanies capitalist social Darwinism.

To explore the possibility that we have the capacity to meet the challenge from our distinctive strengths, it is worthwhile returning to Shoshanna Zuboff's study of trends in advanced high-tech work.[1] Here we get a glimpse of "doing it right"—as well as the obstacles confronted in trying to bring it off. The central issue, as noted earlier in her projection of two scenarios, is the decision whether to *automate* or *informate*. What will be the future of work and power in the "age of the smart machine"? By unveiling the processes emerging in the nature of high-tech work, Zuboff attempts to clarify the choices faced by modern work designers and managers. The fact is that high-tech procedures demand a new quality of "intellective" skill in the work force. And to get that skill requires a transformation of the command tradition of management—moves in a less hierarchical direction. This shift may be threatening. In fact the language and mind-set of organizational designers tend to make them leery of tapping the potential of intellectual skill. It may lead to the loss of the managerial prerogatives. Let us turn now to Zuboff's account of the drama unfolding. As the century ends, the mind-set of American management is still in the grip of the military metaphors of the original designer of factory-type production: Frederick W. Taylor, who spoke of captains of industry and foot soldiers of labor. Even today the fundamental image of work is still seen as a manufacturing enterprise. Raw materials are transformed by machines and physical labor. The technical engineering experts in collaboration with management use their ingenuity and power to design the technology and detailed divisions of labor. It is a dual system of command control. The experts do the thinking; the workers execute prescribed tasks at command. Power is focused in a clear and unquestioned way. A foreman in a Flint, Michigan, auto plant told me: "When I became 'management' I put on the white shirt and tie—and had the authority to kick ass."

This model was refined at mid-century by the veterans who had led the massive victories against Germany and Japan. In the 1950s, America was at the zenith of its mastery of industrial mass production. The corporations leading the charge were organized like military hierarchies with chains of command, job classifications, and standard operating procedures to guide every decision. The emphasis was on establishing control with discipline and standards enforced by detailed supervision. It was an effective approach for that era.

Zuboff goes on to explain how work in the age of the smart machine gets transformed by the emergence of an electronic text. It makes possible two responses that can determine corporate design. On the one hand, there is its potential for expanding and refining the control model with new power of precision. This supports the strategy to *automate*. Its logic moves in the direction of the robotized factory completely devoid of workers—where the physical efforts of humans have been completely transferred to technology. The robotized factory becomes the perfectly controlled facility designed to produce the perfect product. It is freed from diversions like collective bargaining and from "externalities" like medical insurance, family leave, and the like.

Or the strategy may show itself in the form of the sophisticated electronic monitoring of airline representatives at work as described in a Ted Koppel program, "Surveillance on the Job." One of the agents told how she worked under a demerit system monitored by a computer. If she spends an average of more than 109 seconds talking to a customer, she gets one demerit. If she spends more than 11 seconds in between customers, she gets two demerits. After 12 seconds, a light flashes on the console of the supervisor, who then comes in with "Anything wrong? May I help you?" Six demerits earns a warning; thirty-six, dismissal. Another agent reported the monitoring of her time between calls, when she was heard saying a swear word to herself. It was evaluated as "evidence of a bad attitude." Some 6 million clerical workers are now being watched by the unblinking Perfect Gaze. Another 4 million technical managerial people are about to be electronically evaluated in the next few years.[2]

On the other hand, the electronic text may be used to *informate* the work force, an option that replaces hierarchical control and narrow divisions of labor. Informating taps the potential for reflective insight, for creative hypothesizing, for collaborative troubleshooting. It supports democratic values of dignity and participation. Zuboff lays out the great opportunity we may lose if we limit the new power of electronics to preserving a factory-type organizational status quo.

To get her point we need to see her view of the *electronic text*. It opens a major new choice: the choice of informating the workplace so that the worker's "intellective skills" may be combined with computer technology to generate new work styles replacing the Taylorist dualism of labor and management. The electronic text makes possible a fundamental shift in the nature of work from action-centered skills to intellective skills. Zuboff describes how computerization can transform the nature of work in high-tech industries like the batch processing of wood pulp and oil refineries and in white-collar settings like the Global Bank of Brazil.

In precomputer work, many skills were based on sentient knowledge of the physical manipulation of production—much of it internalized in the tacit knowledge of the workers who, in Michael Polanyi's words, "knew more than they could tell." "In a world in which skills were honed over long years of physical experience, work was associated with concrete objects and the cues they provided. A worker's sense of occupational identity was deeply marked by his or her understanding of and attachment to discrete tangible entities, such as a piece of operating equipment."[3] With computerization, this personal knowledge is abstracted and transferred to the electronic text. For some workers, it is as if a job has vanished into a two-dimensional space of abstractions where digital symbols replace concrete reality.

The information text is built up by incorporating the whole range of skills and processes that constitute the production system. In paper mills, "procedures and informal knowledge can be codified and built into the structure of an information system, thus increasing the depth of a text. For example, benefit analysts were debriefed, and their knowledge was built into the design of the system; the skilled operators were debriefed, and their knowledge contributed to the programs that automated aspects of the production process; and managers were debriefed and their methods of utilizing information were designed into the structure of the data base."[4] This relentless extraction of information makes for powerful centralization and an equally radical decentralization. In principle, the electronic text can be constituted or called up at any time from any place and its contents can be made available throughout the entire organization.

This powerful information technology can be used to automate. It can reproduce, extend, and improve the process of substituting machines for human labor. It can even automate the production of robots, so that robots produce robots. But it opens other possibilities as well. The electronic devices that link information to action can simultaneously register data about these automated functionings, thereby producing new streams of information. For example, scanner devices in supermarkets automate the checkout job. But they simultaneously generate data that can be used for inventory control, orders from warehouses, scheduling of deliveries, and market analysis.

In this kind of performance, the electronic system that makes possible automating also creates an overview of the total organization's operations, with many levels of data coordinated and made accessible for analytical efforts. What is new is that this information technology which may automate an activity also *produces* information while doing so. It both accomplishes tasks (automates) and translates them into information (informates). The action of a *machine* is entirely directed to production of its product. Information technology, on the other hand, introduces an additional dimension of reflexivity: It makes its contribution to the product, but it also reflects back on its activities and on the system of activities to which it is related. Information technology not only produces action but also produces a voice that symbolically renders events, objects, and processes so that they become visible, knowable, and shareable in a new way.

Seen in this way, the fundamental duality inherent in information technology becomes clear. If the technology is treated narrowly in its automating function, it merely perpetuates the logic of the industrial machine which, during the twentieth century, has made it possible to rationalize work and reduce dependence on human skills. But if its potential to *informate* is tapped, it can release dynamics that may reconfigure the nature of work and the social relations in productive activity.

The Electronic Text and the Work Force

In helping us to see the profound way in which work may be transformed, Zuboff contrasts the nature of action-centered skills of industrialism with the intellective skills that emerge with the electronic text. Action-centered skills require a detailed understanding of the physical medium in which work is done. Workers involved in the transition talk about their work skills being rooted in an ability to see things to which they can make an immediate physical response—a "cause and effect" kind of knowledge, one that grows out of concrete experiences with materials, tools, and situations and becomes internalized into "tacit knowledge."

With computerization, immediate physical responses are replaced by abstract thought as control of physical production is incorporated into "the smart machine." One worker described his personal disorientation in experiencing the shift:

> Our operators did their job by feeling a pipe— "Is it hot?" We can't just tell them it's 150 degrees. They have to believe it.
>
> With computerization I am further away from my job than I have ever been before. I used to listen to the sounds the boiler makes and know

> just how it was running. I could look at the fire
> in the furnace and tell by its color how it was
> burning. I knew what kinds of adjustments were
> needed by the shades of color I saw. A lot of the
> men also said that there were smells that told you
> different things about how it was running. I feel
> uncomfortable being away from these sights and
> smells. Now I only have numbers to go by. I am
> scared of that boiler, and I feel that I should be
> closer to it in order to control it.[5]

With the introduction of computerization, workers are asked
to leave behind a world in which things are immediately
known and can be acted upon directly. They enter a world
dominated by objective data that demand a qualitatively different response. One manager described the transition: "Once
we put things under automatic control and ask them to relate
to the process using the computer, their personal judgments
about how to relate to equipment go by the wayside. We are
saying your intuition is no longer valuable. Now you must
understand the whole process and the theory behind it."[6]

When hammers and wrenches are displaced by numbers
and buttons, a whole new kind of learning must begin—and
it can be scary. We are at the point where action-centered
skills must be replaced by intellective skills. After introduction
of the electronic text, operators must first think about what
has to be done; they must know how data correspond to
actual processes and relations in the system. To do that operators have to understand the information system itself, so
that after deciding what to do they can scan new data and
check for results—a kind of thinking that can stand independent from the physical operation.

Zuboff reports that some paper mill operators, for example, found the change too threatening and quit. The majority,
however, became intrigued with the new opportunities—savor-
ing the discovery of their unexpected abilities to handle the challenges of a more strictly intellectual effort. An operator who had
been transferred to a newly computerized operation observed:

If something is happening, if something is going
wrong, you don't go down and fix it. Instead you
stay up here and think about the sequence. You
get it done through your thinking. But dealing
with information instead of things is very . . .
well, very intriguing. . . . Things occur to me
now that never would have occurred to me. I
begin to think about how to do the job better.
And, being freed from all that manual activity,
you really have time to look at things, to think
about them, and to anticipate.[7]

The operator is pointing to the fact that a kind of learning is
required, one which demands the constructing of meaning
from symbols. When people confront the electronic text and
ask "What is happening? What does that mean?" the answers
frequently require a sharing of hypotheses and insights to
secure the best interpretation of the text.

Zuboff reports that in her observations the interpre-
tations developed by operators and managers were often
constructed through dialogue and hypothesis testing. One
operator described the process:

If there is a problem, everyone gets together and
figures it out. There might be umpteen things it
could be. . . . You cannot take a book and find
out exactly how this computer works. It is not
like that. It is the sort of thing where we have to
put our knowledge together in order to understand what it is doing, and what it should be
doing. . . . We all get involved in the problem, so
we all know what happens. A couple of people
stay at the terminal, and a couple go out and
check things. First, we all look it over on the computer. Then, you see what you need to do outside.
Or, if there's little time, someone runs to the door,
and the person at the terminal will yell "Check
this and that" while you're running out the door.[8]

Thus both managers and workers are seeing the need for sociality—the new technology can bring people together, people who understand the electronics, the programming, and the information complexity. In coming together they need to discuss what they see, what they know and understand, and what should be done. Is it straining too much to say that, in Gadamer's terms, they have become dialogical constructors of meaning?

As the concept of integrated production grows in importance, the web of communication for effective performance expands. This showed up in Zuboff's observation of developments at the Global Bank of Brazil as computerization integrated data across all banking functions. The old functional organization that separated people into neatly defined specialties was brought into question. Managers began to see that integration of the data base required collaboration of the various functions—in order to generate new ideas for profitability. They began to see that the data-base environment had become one information system for all to see. It then became possible to see the whole—which led one manager to suggest that because everyone is looking at the same data, and everyone is selling products, the current delineations between operations, credit, and marketing were becoming counterproductive. The vision that emerged was of a group of people with a variety of skills who could be brought together around the data base. They could collaborate on a construction of meaning that would lead to new opportunities for innovation. A manager described the data base as the "vault" that contained its bank's real assets. Intellectual mastery and teamwork would provide the keys to the vault.

When the electronic text leads to viewing the processing in this way, the whole concept of what is involved in good work begins to undergo a transformation. Learning becomes a top priority. Managers begin to see that workers need access to data so they can analyze and understand the system so they can troubleshoot and innovate. As one operator said, "If I can control my own access to data, I can control my own learning." Beyond that an organizational climate is required that supports the essential conditions of a learning environment: freedom to play, experiment, and enter into dialogue.[9]

High-tech industries adopting an informating rationale are finding that tapping the brains of people at work yields new levels of effectiveness. But at a cost, too, that can be threatening to management. The technology that informates the work force can have a corrosive effect on the hierarchical organization. When the information of the electronic text is made accessible to the work force, the logic of Taylorism is undermined. The knowledge that had been extracted from workers and given to the "Taylors" is now returned to the workers—but with a difference. There is a kind of knowledge in the electronic text, external to the workers, that they must grapple with and reappropriate as their own to gain meaning and insight. They need to develop the intellective skills appropriate for the electronic text. The goal of the informating process is to maximize the results that can be secured by learning in the situation. Making the organization more transparent can promote communal insight. Seen in this way, access to new data, new events, and new contexts creates opportunities for further insights, improvements, and innovations. A learning environment is required that encourages questions and dialogue and collegial relationships that support intellectual interaction and exploration.

The boundaries that used to define managerial knowledge begin to blur. To maximize the potential of automating, the intellective skills of the work force have to be supported—and the central strategy for doing so becomes the redefinition of the system of authority. The manager who asked "Are we all going to be working for a smart machine, or will we have smart people around the machine?" defined the critical choices faced by management.[10] The first choice leads to computer-based automation with the industrial-era goal: to establish managerial control over the knowledge base and to engineer a division of labor that deskills a shrinking work force—the latest effort to consolidate managerial authority. When the workers resist, the response is to sink more resources into automation and supervision. It is the lure of panopticon power strengthened now by electronic surveillance. Zuboff describes case after case where management flinched when faced with the choice of *informating* (and strengthening competitiveness) or *automating* (and consolidating control with loss of effectiveness). Management chose machine intelligence and managerial control over creating the more egalitarian, interactive learning environment that would capitalize on the intellective skills of workers.

But Zuboff reports important exceptions where management and workers were choosing the learning environment required for informating. A difficult cultural shift is involved, and the challenges should not be underestimated. When management realizes that the dual separation of thinking from executing that characterizes classic management is not only outmoded but dysfunctional, the way opens for exploring alternatives to hierarchy—management faces the fact that learning is the productive heart of an informated work "place" where information circulates and must be responded to with thinking. A "division of learning" replaces the division of labor, one that takes on a new vocabulary: colearners, exploration, experimentation, innovation. Such an informating strategy can lead to a new distribution of knowledge and authority that permits many to contribute and negates old status boundaries.

The relationships that emerge can be thought of as posthierarchical. The old organization aimed for well-controlled functioning under hierarchical authority. People related to each other in predictable ways prescribed by rank and status. Management acted *on* the organization to secure effective functioning. In an informating setting, however, new demands are made on management. Relationships vary more in terms of what people know and feel and what the task at hand requires. Relationships operate more flexibly as people participate in processes, such as inquiry and dialogue, that support learning. To be effective, managers need *acting-with* skills—skills that sustain morale, motivation, and commitment to get work done in conditions of change. The skills needed are those appropriate for post-hierarchical relationships.

Not everyone is able or willing to play in this new world. For management the threats are obvious. The old command style becomes dysfunctional. Job security itself can be threatened. A thinning out of middle-level management occurs where autonomous work teams are given responsibility for supervision and monitoring quality control. Moreover, some workers view the apparent new freedoms with suspicion, fear, and even despair. These negative reactions come in different forms.

Some cherish the sense of autonomy they got when their special skills were protected by the union contract. To relinquish well-defined job descriptions for immersion into a socially integrated high-tech workplace may make them vulnerable to the whims of their superiors. And there are always those for whom psychological distance is important. Then, too, even if some work is brought under a participative informating strategy other jobs will remain routine or become automated. Thus new questions of equity arise. Finally, there are the concerns of unions—many of them well founded. Will "the happy feeling" of participative management create a wedge between workers and the union? The shrinkage of union membership in the eighties can be attributed in large part to the shift from industrial to service employment. But the fact is that new plant start-ups with high worker participation have often been designed with an eye to avoiding unionization. And in many cases they have been successful. Even where unions remain in place, traditional roles of union officials from shop stewards on up are brought under question for redefinition.

While these and other consequences can be disturbing, the potential for alternatives to Taylorist manipulation and control cannot be denied. In Zuboff's study the informating strategy that combines high technology with constructivist-style learning and values from our democratic tradition turns out to be best for successful competition in the international market. It opens, too, the possibility of a moral alternative to our long attachment to the demoralizing tenets of Taylorism. For economic survival, people at work have to be treated in terms of their higher human capacities and not as hired hands. We hear once more an echo of the words of economist Hazel Henderson: "For the first time in history, morality has become pragmatic."[11]

Farewell to Industrial Mass Production

Robert Reich, in *The Work of Nations: Preparing Ourselves for 21st Century Capitalism*,[12] offers another dimension of the transformation of work that explains the need to choose informating over automating. His point is that the 1950s model of industrial mass production is moving toward dinosaur-type obsolescence. The reason is the shift from high-volume production to high-value production. There are two basic forces behind this shift: the rush of product changes that accompany computer-assisted production and service and the complex diversity of needs in the world market where business must now be done.

Reich argues that the modern corporation at the end of the twentieth century only superficially resembles its 1950 counterpart. In the first place, the huge national corporations of yesteryear that were famous for mass-produced products like rubber tires, radios, and automobiles are progressively being transformed into international corporations with offices and personnel located all over the world. (Some 40 percent of IBM employees are from foreign lands.) Their products are international composites with components with worldwide networks of production, research, finance, and marketing. Thus ice hockey equipment distributed in North America may be designed in Sweden, financed in Canada, assembled in Denmark out of alloys researched and patented in Delaware, and manufactured in Japan; a space satellite launched by a rocket in the USSR is designed in California, manufactured in France, and financed by Australians. Real-world corporations, instead of looking like massive monoliths, increasingly look like an array of decentralized units (or subunits) continuously contracting with similarly diffuse working units all over the world.

Under the pressures of diverse customer demand and the challenge of world competitors, transformations are taking place often by fits and starts, not always consciously planned. American corporations finding that they can no longer generate large earnings from high-volume production of standard commodities are gradually turning toward serving the special needs of unique customers. They are surviving by shifting from high-volume to high-value production. Other worldwide corporations are doing the same thing. The biggest profits in chemicals, for example, come from specialty chemicals designed for specific industrial uses. In plastics, profits no longer flow from large batches of basic polymers but from special polymers created from unique combinations of molecules that can withstand a wide range of stress and temperature and be molded into intricate parts. Older industries like textiles that survive are those that produce specialty coated and finished fabrics for cars, rain gear, and office furniture. Tool and die casters stay viable by making precision aluminum and zinc castings for computer frames, inserts, and disk-drive components. Profitable semiconductor firms make specialized microprocessors and customized chips tailored for diverse customers.

Traditional services are going through a similar transformation. Thus the high profits in telecommunications derive from long-distance services like voice, video, and information processing and from telecommunication networks that link employees in different locations by facsimile machines, computers, and phones.

For successful internationally oriented corporations, the key skill is in finding the right fit between particular technologies and particular markets. This means that strategies increasingly center on specialized knowledge—and those that have it or produce it. New transitional work is made possible by a global communication network utilizing computers, facsimile machines, satellites, high-resolution monitors, and modems that link engineers, designers, contractors, and dealers worldwide.

This global system, which is in a constant state of change and refinement, is made possible not only by evolving technology but also by a set of key human skills that are the source of value for high-value enterprises. It is a socio(human)-technical system. Reich says there are three different but related skills that drive it forward. First are the problem-solving skills required to put things together in unique ways, whether they be molecules, alloys, semiconductor chips, pension portfolios, or information. These are the skills used by employees who are continually searching for new combinations and refinements capable of solving all kinds of emerging problems.

Second are skills required to help customers decide how their shifting needs can best be met by customized products. This requires an intimate knowledge of customers' whole operations and how they may achieve a competitive advantage. The key is to identify new problems and possibilities that may relate to their customized products.

Third are skills needed to link the problem solvers and problem identifiers. These people must understand specific technologies and markets to see the potential for new products and how to assemble the problem solvers and identifiers to carry it out. Their special skill is in managing ideas and bringing the right people together for creative action.

These new high-value enterprises cannot function with the old bureaucratic, pyramid-style organization where various layers of managers and supervisors are combined with obedient hourly workers, all aimed at following standard operating procedures. In what Reich calls "the new work of enterprise," the three groups—problem solvers, problem identifiers, and strategic brokers—need to be in constant communication to discover new opportunities and get the right answers for the right problems at the right time.

Reich says that with these developments a new skill category is emerging beyond the routine production and service work skills. These are the skills of what he calls symbolic analysis. Symbolic analysts are people who solve, identify, and broker problems by manipulating symbols. They translate reality into abstract images that can be juggled, experimented with, and communicated to other specialists. Their analytic tools may be scientific principles, mathematical algorithms, psychological insights, financial schemes, or any techniques useful for obtaining product or service improvements. They are engineers of various types (design, software, biotechnology), research scientists, consultants (on energy, management, agriculture, taxes, architecture), management information specialists, system analysts, and others.

They operate with a distinctive work style. Often they work with associates or partners rather than under bosses. They may work alone or with small teams connected to the international networks. Since neither problems nor solutions are known in advance, they communicate constantly, often informally, to see that insights are put to best use and ideas are evaluated quickly and critically. They produce plans, designs, drafts, layouts, scripts, or projections based on their skill in conceptualizing problems and solutions.

So far the opportunities for those with symbolic-analytic skills have mainly been for people who design and make decisions regarding production. But there is ample evidence that access to computerized information can enlarge production and service jobs as well. Workers with access to computer data can change the flow of production and later modify components to develop new efficiencies. If provided with an informating environment, production workers can gain more control over how production is organized. As they cease to be "routine workers," they become symbolic analysts at the center of the production process.

The same holds for people in face-to-face service jobs. For example, the computer now enables the checkout clerk to control inventory and make decisions when to reorder from the factory. Thus the clerk is empowered to assume more responsibility and add more value to the enterprise. To be capable of performing such upgraded work, however, the clerk must be capable of learning on the job—and this means a firm grounding in reading and communication skills as well as mathematics and basic science.

The growing demand worldwide is for workers with symbolic-analytic skills. Witness the foreign students swarming into American universities. What kind of learning is required to produce symbolic analysts? At the heart of it Reich says we need a formal education that will refine four basic skills: abstraction, system thinking, experimentation, and collaboration.

First, the capacity for *abstraction* is marked by the ability to discover patterns and meaning. Complex reality must be simplified and grasped so that it can be manipulated in new ways. The symbolic analyst employs analogies, models, constructs, formulas, categories, and metaphors to create possibilities for rearranging the chaotic swirl of data. Information itself is inadequate. What is needed are the abstract thinking skills that can shape raw data into workable patterns. Prepackaged lessons and textbooks that impose meanings on students deny them the practice of *constructing* meaning.

Second, *system thinking* extends abstraction one step further. Industrial-type education, 1950 style, tends to present the world as composed of discrete components, each of which can be learned in isolation. Symbolic analysts, however, whose task is to see new possibilities, must be able to understand the processes by which parts of reality are linked together. They must be able to discern larger patterns, causal connections, relationships, consequences. A symbolic analyst can see that the problem of designing safe landfills may be abetted by the invention and use of biodegradable containers.

Third, symbolic analysts need the skills of critical *experimental inquiry* to put ideas to the test. They need the skills of testing hypotheses, observing, comprehending causes and consequences, and drawing conclusions as to which ideas, in John Dewey's term, can be accepted as "warranted assertions." Advanced forms of experimentation do not follow neat formulas. They often entail false starts, frustration, and fear. Symbolic analysts are constantly experimenting: The design engineer tries out new materials for engine parts; the ecological planner explores which course of action minimizes damage to the environment. The habits and methods of experimentation are critical in the new economy, where technologies and markets are in constant flux. Schooling that focuses sharply on the accumulation of right answers misses the mark and is even dysfunctional.

Finally, there is the capacity to *collaborate.* Symbolic analysts typically work in teams, where their style of exploring problems and solutions is not unrelated to the playlike quality of good preschool learning. They also have to communicate and collaborate in preparing meaningful reports, presentations, layouts, designs, and projections. In the process, they are employing abstract concepts and learning to achieve consensus. This is a very different picture from classrooms that get high performance ratings by rules which say "No talking," "No passing of notes," "No giving of help" because the goal is to excel by individual performance.

Shoshanna Zuboff and Robert Reich show us the choices faced by leaders of American industry and labor in plotting strategies for survival in the turbulent world of high technology and international competition. By the choices they make, these leaders will be deciding the quality of life and learning that Americans will experience in their daily work. Reich's analysis establishes that the style and content of learning in American schools are directly involved in these choices.

Six

The Business Perspective on Schooling: A Mixed Message

If we turn to what was happening in American education as the country entered the 1990s, it is not surprising to find parallel tensions to those in industry. The top-down bureaucratic control model, reinforced by state prescriptions, was still a potent force, but it was being challenged. President Bush's new secretary of education, Lauro Cavazos, acknowledged the growing disillusionment with the first phase of reform: "We tried to improve education by imposing regulations from the top down, while leaving the basic structure of the school untouched. Obviously that hasn't worked."[1]

A similar sentiment had been expressed as early as 1985 in a report by the Committee for Economic Development (CED) entitled *Investing in Our Children: Business and the Public Schools.* The motivation once again grew out of industry's concern about survival in global competition. In this report, leaders of industries that are being transformed by technology appear to be supporting the informating style and the skills of the symbolic analyst. But, as we shall see, they unwittingly vitiate that style by recommendations from the

71

"bottom line" mind-set of the business culture. Let us first follow the argument of the executives and then examine the complexities of school testing.

What the CED Found

The co-directors of *Investing in Our Children* were Denis P. Doyle and Marsha Levine of the conservative American Enterprise Institute. Listed on various committees of the Committee for Economic Development are people like Owen Butler, chairman of Procter & Gamble; Ralph Lazarus, head of Federated Department Stores; William Woodside, chairman of American Can Co.; Robert Davenport, head of Sheridan Broadcasting Co.; Roger Smith, chairman of General Motors; and Thomas Vanderslice, president of Apollo Computer, Inc. From education one finds well-known figures like Harold Howe, former U.S. commissioner of education; Albert Shanker, president of the American Federation of Teachers; and John Brademas, president of New York University. The project on education followed a major CED study of American economic productivity which concluded that economic productivity and the quality of education cannot be separated. Their studies of Asian and European competitors demonstrated to the CED that human resources are more important than physical ones, and that a work force educated simply by "old school basics" will not be equipped for meeting the challenges of turbulent change.

They presented the case of Procter & Gamble to make their point. In the past, workers joined Procter & Gamble to enter low-skilled tasks in narrowly defined jobs—which changed little during a person's work life. The strong trend now is toward participative work systems. Employees perform a broad range of tasks including operating and maintaining equipment and performing their own quality control. They participate in activities, such as goal setting and budgeting, formerly reserved strictly for management. Increasingly work is performed by self-directed teams where problem solving and decision making are important parts of the job. The company provides retraining in the high-level skills needed to meet the flow of change. Training is effective only if employees have strong literacy and number skills, and above all the ability to learn. With this as their conception of new work, they issued a call for "nothing less than a revolution in the role of the teacher and the management of schools."

High-tech firms, they say, are not served well by old organizational forms. Centralized rigid bureaucracies, whether in schools or industry, are hostile to creativity. They stifle it because their goal is to keep control in the hands of centralized authority. The essential obligation of organizations in the new era, however, is "to nurture creativity." Schools (and previous national reports on schools) have neglected this fact. School policymakers must learn the lesson of industry—to relegate decision making to the lowest possible level: "Solve the problem where it exists." Give employees a stake in the system by letting them exercise their own creativity and energy in the work at hand. Specifically, the report recommends a bottom-up policy for school reform. Focus is on the individual school as the key place for meaningful improvement in quality and productivity. The role of the states, they say, is to give top-down guidance and support by setting clear goals and high standards—and then giving the schools the maximum freedom to implement them.[2]

The interaction of teachers, students, and administrators in individual schools becomes the key arena for action. The report assumes that the able, sensitive, highly professional school people now needed will not choose teaching, nor choose to remain in it, if they are stifled by present bureaucratic regimentation or shackled with "teacher-proof" materials. Teachers will respond only if their professional roles are enhanced by opportunities to exercise judgment, make decisions, and reshape their own working environment. Teachers may be surprised to find, the report says, that contrary to the narrow "back to basics" emphasis of recent years, the CED calls for liberal education for all: for higher-order learning—to think critically and analytically, to cooperate and communicate as well as to compete, to solve problems, to assume responsibility, and to learn to learn. They advocate "teacher centers" where peers can exchange ideas on strategies for advancing learning and changing "the culture of the school." Where teacher evaluation is concerned, they shy away from merit plans that often undermine collegial relations. Teachers working in a largely competitive environment, they say, will be less inclined to support the sense of community that is essential for effective schools.

This hasty sketch illustrates that these corporate leaders now accept Zuboff's Scenario II with its informating and decentralization as the way of the future. But the contradictions between this new perspective on schools and the assumptions of the business world soon become apparent.

Where the CED Went Wrong

Various corporate units in industry, the CED report says, are given a great deal of autonomy on how they organize themselves so long as they meet corporate directives: "Decentralization works because the results can be measured." While admitting that schools are not the same as industry, the report insists that the outcomes of schooling can and must be measured. States should look to output measures, rather than process requirements, to hold schools accountable. The formula seems reasonable enough: "Invest in schools to get a good return on your investment. States, like industries, should look to bottom-line numbers—to get output measures to hold schools accountable." The relevant "output measures" in 1985 were standardized test scores.

The problem with such statements is not that they are devoid of good intentions, but that they slip into the mistaken idea that measuring productivity in industry is analogous to producing measurable units of children's learning in schools. They assume that educators have tools of measurement comparable to the tools of engineers in industry. It is a sadly mistaken assumption. As John Goodlad, one of the most serious students of American education, has pointed out, the whole effort to rationalize instruction as in industry ignores the fact that there is no science of education "sufficient to give credence to the 'scientism' necessary for these quantifiable accountability models."[3] And we do not get such a science simply by saying we must have one. If we nevertheless continue to measure as if the science existed, we are out of touch with reality. When that happens we are in trouble.

The real issue is whether you can make standardized test scores the central criterion for judging the effectiveness of teachers without undermining those other "new goals": for teachers, autonomy and creativity; for students, collaborative learning, divergent thinking, and higher-order conceptual skills; for symbolic analysts, the ability to handle complexity with abstract analysis, the capacity for holistic thinking, the capacity to confront the problematic with the skills of experimental inquiry, and the ability to communicate and collaborate by means of new technology and dialogue.

When corporate executives have been conditioned by a lifetime of learning that the critical factor is the number on the bottom line, it seems hardly surprising that they think "states should look to outcome measures to hold schools accountable." What they may have trouble comprehending is that the instruments available for mass usage are standardized tests that put enormous pressures on schools to stay locked in the industrial mode of 1950s schooling. The educational system of the fifties fit nicely the structure of high-volume corporate production. American schools then mirrored the national economy with a standard curriculum divided neatly into subjects, taught in prescribed units of time, arranged sequentially by grade levels, and controlled by standardized tests.

Despite talk about creativity, higher-order thinking, collaborative learning, and bold innovation, high-stakes testing pressures schools into 1950-style standardization in order to pass muster on the standardized tests. If the results seem unsatisfactory, the only option seems to be to do more of the same— to see that standardized tests become even more determinative of what will be poured into the resistant noggins of the young. It is time to bring under scrutiny the phenomenon of testing called "the linchpin" of school reform of the early 1980s.

Seven

Testing:
Cure or Curse?

The insistence of the business sector that school reform be made accountable in terms of standardized test results points to one of the most complex and troubling aspects of efforts at public school improvement. The dilemma may be stated as follows: On the one hand, it seems reasonable to ask for evidence of educational results, and standardized test scores seem to be the answer. Industry, after all, has to show bottom-line numbers. On the other hand, what if the industry metaphor of treating education as a production function not only does not fit school reality but, in fact, is harmful to it? The choice then is between insisting on easily administered testing as *the* instrument of accountability, even if injurious, or challenging the assumptions behind it and seeking forms of assessment that support the kind of learning really needed.

While I am a critic of the current obsession with test score accountability, I am willing to concede that there is no simple answer. We are confronted with a class of two competing goods: the right to know if our children are learning versus the need to ensure the integrity of learning and teaching. Indeed, creative teachers insist that high-stakes testing forces them to be part of a fraudulent system that appears to produce significant learning while undermining the real thing. To confront these complexities, let us begin with an effort to give a hearing to both sides. Since I am a critic of the overuse of standardized testing, I shall include a critique and point to some alternative ideas that are emerging.

The Trouble with Standardized Testing

A marked increase in testing began in the mid 1970s. Testing provisions had been included earlier in federal and state educational reform legislation—in, for example, the post-*Sputnik* National Defense Education Act of 1958, in the Elementary and Secondary Education Act of 1965, and in the Rehabilitation Act of 1973. Senator Robert Kennedy, a leading proponent of Johnson-era legislation to improve the quality of education for minority children, argued that black parents have a right to know if their children are in fact learning.

In the late 1970s and early 1980s, a variety of forces gave new impetus to a movement for test score accountability. There was a growing concern about a drop in test scores and, as we entered the 1980s, a parallel concern about America's ability to meet global competition from the thriving Japanese and European economies. One response was a rush of legislation by the states with mandated curriculum and testing prescriptions to restore "excellence." A powerful force behind the trend was a new involvement by the business community.

The business world, worried about effects on its competitiveness of an inadequately educated work force, began to demand the kind of accountability of educators that they said was expected of themselves. The culture of business leaders is bottom-line oriented. They thought that the instrument for securing objective numbers in education was standardized tests. They assumed that these tests measure the knowledge that educated products are expected to have. Test scores could be trusted more than subjective teacher judgments.

William Bennett, President Reagan's secretary of education, gave his imprimatur in declaring that test score accountability is the linchpin of educational reform. There were claims of vindication when a variety of reports of test score improvements came in. Eventually, however, unanticipated consequences emerged that cast doubt on what seemed to be the road to victory. Critics began to speak out.

One charge was that high-stakes testing was having corrupting effects on testing itself, and on the process of learning and teacher morale in schools. When teachers' salaries and comparative school ratings are based on test score results, those scores will go up. Dr. John Cannell, in his report *How All Fifty States Are Above the National Average,* pointed out in 1987 that school systems across the country, including impoverished inner-city systems, were reporting that they were above the norm. "All systems above the norm" is undoubtedly a remarkable achievement. When Garrison Keillor reported the phenomenon's appearance in Lake Woebegon, it became known as the "Lake Woebegon" effect—"the women are strong, the men good-looking, and all the children are above average." Cannell's conclusions were disputed, but the National Commission on Testing and Public Policy (1990) reported that other studies confirmed his suspicions: Test results across the nation are inflated. Moreover, troubling school practices have emerged in response to the pressures: aligning instruction with test content, teaching to the test, teaching the test itself, using tests meant for children at a lower grade, exempting low achievers, and outright fraud and cheating.[1]

In poverty-stricken St. Louis, teachers' salary differences were attached to student test performance. Predictably, scores went up, but complaints emerged about teachers teaching for the test—or worse. A school board member responded by offering his telephone as a hot line where students, teachers, and staff members could report anonymously any suspicions they might have. Scores went up, teacher morale went down, and students were learning more than standardized test knowledge. They were learning that their teachers, resenting a system they do not believe in, will cheat.

A fundamental source of distortion came from adopting the prevailing metaphor of schooling as a production line—with the assumption that schools can produce a specified product with quality control through testing. Such thinking is out of touch with the complex reality of human learning. One result of such a mistaken effort, said Dr. Roger C. Schank of Northwestern's Institute for Learning Sciences, is that American education has become too "right-answer oriented" and discourages thinking. "Over the years," he says, "the quality of our school system has been deteriorating as the people running them have concentrated more and more on test results. We have gotten more interested in standardized tests, tests have become more standardized, and our schools have gotten worse. It's all related."[2]

A more detailed bill of particulars came in a May 1990 report of the National Commission on Testing and Public Policy, *From Gatekeeper to Gateway: Transforming Testing in America.* The research, financed by a $750,000 grant from the Ford Foundation, was directed by George Madaus, director of Boston College's Study of Testing, Evaluation, and Educational Policy. This three-year study included a review of research of more than 100 scholars and consultation with Secretary of Education Lauro F. Cavazos and White House and congressional advisers. It cited the major limitations of testing: Tests are imperfect and can mislead one about a student's potential for education and work; they can lead to unfair treatment of individuals and groups; they can undermine policies intended to develop and use human talent; and, finally, the companies that design tests have not been held to public accountability.[3] The report also supported the critics who say there is too much testing. According to the report, mandatory testing consumes annually some 20 million school days and the equivalent of $700 and $900 million in direct and indirect expenditures. By 1990, all states had mandatory testing programs as compared to only one state in 1972.[4]

The costs were more than monetary. Madaus said that high-stakes testing eventually determines the curriculum: What is not emphasized on the tests is not emphasized in schools. When emphasis is placed on high scores in reading and arithmetic, for example, social studies, science, and the arts may get neglected. A national study by the Center for Research in Mathematical Science Education concluded that teachers who concentrate on teaching for standardized tests do so at a tremendous sacrifice. They neglect the intellectual engagement that students need in order to develop the mathematical abilities recommended by the National Council of Teachers of Mathematics.[5]

A RAND study described the effects of school policies based on test scores of basic skills. Teachers reported that the time for "real teaching" was diminished sharply by time devoted to preparing for tests, giving the tests, and keeping records related to test objectives. Teachers saw the "real teaching" they wanted to do as related to nontested modes of thinking and doing—reading books, writing, discussing ideas, and projects involving research, creative activities, and inductive problem solving. Because such activities take a lot of time and do not lend themselves to measurement, they give way to a focus on the basic skills that are more easily tested.

A 1991 study of elementary teachers in Arizona found that when test results were publicly reported they induced in teachers anxiety, shame, loss of esteem, and alienation. In response, teachers became determined to do whatever it took to raise scores. One result was that they devoted about 100 hours previously allocated to instruction to preparing for tests and administering them. When there was a discrepancy between their curriculum goals and the skills that the test measured, the teachers reduced more complex content such as math problem solving to computational skills and reduced broader writing and language skills to punctuation. The investigator concluded that teaching itself had become testlike. Teachers became deskilled as "multiple-choice testing led to multiple-choice teaching."[6] Another study in California showed how a curriculum reform like a new California mathematics program, aimed at higher-order thinking skills, can get overpowered when it runs up against a mandated skills testing program. The test wins out. In one teacher's words,

"Teaching for understanding is what we are supposed to be doing . . . [but] the bottom line here is that all they really want to know is, how are these kids doing on the tests? . . . They want me to teach in a way that they can't test, except that I'm held accountable to the test."[7]

Apart from showing the negative effects of testing on the integrity of teaching and learning, the National Commission pointed to another major reason for changing test policies: "Our central finding is that current practices in educational and employment testing stand in the way of efforts to identify and develop talent, and to improve the functioning of key social institutions. . . . Only recently are the unintended negative results of using tests as instruments of policy becoming clear."[8] Behind this statement is the realization that America now is confronted with a crucial social change. The country's entry-level work force is shrinking and is increasingly composed of linguistic, racial, and cultural minority groups whose talents have often been underdeveloped and undervalued. (For example: The portion of the population under the age of thirty-five is expected to drop from its present 55 percent to 41 percent by the year 2030. The nonwhite work force is expected to increase by 45 percent by 2010.)[9] By the year 2000, one-third of all children in the United States will be nonwhite compared to one-fifth in 1988.[10]

The poor and the nonwhite often score low on standardized testing. Women, who will make up more than half of the work force by the year 2000, score lower than men on certain important tests such as college entrance examinations—yet often perform better in school than men. Nonwhites score significantly lower as a group, but the factors responsible are so complex that research has only meagerly begun to understand it. The simple idea that current standardized tests yield objective scientific facts about learning differences, and that kids who score lower are dumber than kids who score higher, is a myth. Some lower scores are due to unequal educational and social opportunities. We do not know how to measure the human effects of poverty; nor do we know the impact of having grown up with a language different from that used in the tests.

Some scores, Madaus says, "reflect bias or unfairness in ways that I don't think statistical tests will ever pick up. We simply don't know enough yet about how and why people answer questions in the ways that they do." One researcher studying how minority populations answer certain types of questions found some children selecting "cabbage" when the test asked "Which needs the least amount of water? A cactus, a geranium, or a cabbage?" These students selected cabbage instead of cactus "because it is already picked." The realization is growing that "no test is reliable and accurate enough to be used by itself for the kinds of high-stakes educational decisions being made."[11] The chairman of the National Commission, Bernard R. Gifford, who is also vice-president for education for Apple Computer, Inc., has said that "traditionally, testing has been used to weed people out of the opportunity market. . . . We're now at the point where this country can't afford to weed people out of opportunities."[12]

Broadening Our Conception of Testing

Part of the problem lies in public misunderstanding of what tests can and cannot do. The report says that tests provide only a small sample of what someone knows or can do at the time of the test; they cannot precisely predict future school or workplace performance. A glaring example was the 1976 error in calibration of the Armed Services Vocational Aptitude Battery (ASVAB) that led to 300,000 recruits being admitted to the military who normally would have been rejected because of low scores. Follow-up studies showed that as a group these enlistees performed only somewhat less well than those who passed the ASVAB, and many did as well or better.

The report concludes not that tests have no role in classifying people, but that it is poor policy to classify *only* on the basis of one imperfect instrument.[13] (The country was willing to trust many of these men with high-tech weaponry in the war in the Persian Gulf.) The present misuse of tests to "weed out" people is self-defeating, says the report. It is time to get on with the democratic goal of asking: How can the results of tests and other assessments be interpreted so that "visions of human potential are enlarged rather than circumscribed? Test scores, by themselves, should never brand anyone as a failure or permanently restrict opportunities. . . . Potentially negative classification in school or the workplace should be accompanied by opportunities for learning."[14]

Another misconception about tests is that one can easily tell how well American educators are doing by comparing U.S. national test scores with those of other countries. As Seymour Sarason, professor of psychology at Yale University, puts it: "The United States is unique in this world in the racial-ethnic-cultural composition of its population, a heterogeneity that in the past and present has no precedent. Indeed in the light of this fantastic heterogeneity one might seek to explain not why our schools are as bad as they are but rather why they are as good as they are."[15] It could be added that a two-year international study by the Joint Center for Political and Economic Studies, a Washington, D.C., research center, reported that the United States has more poverty and is coping with it less well than any of the other major industrialized democracies.[16] And test scores are correlated closely with levels of income.

Factors like these cannot responsibly be passed over. Positing high goals to make people reach higher is commendable, but it can be demoralizing when reality is ignored. As Marc Tucker, president of the National Center for Education and the Economy, remarked: "The math and science goal is critical, but reaching it with 20 percent of our kids in poverty is ludicrous."[17] Tests *can* give a lot of useful information. Much depends on the use we want to make of them. If we believe human beings in general are curious about the world and want to learn, we will use tests not primarily to sort out winners from losers, but to identify the areas where individuals could benefit from remediation programs that may help bring them in as useful members of the polis.

Where does that leave us with respect to the role of

testing? It leaves us with a complex conflicted issue that reflects deep value cleavages in American society. A constructive course has yet to be designed. On the one hand, it is no longer arguable that standardized tests give us objective facts about who is dumb or smart. On the other hand, critics must recognize the legitimacy of citizens' requests to know the results of teaching and educational effort. George Madaus, for example, accepts that tests in some form will have a role to play as broader forms of evaluation are created. There are opportunities for creative innovations as the whole concept of evaluation and testing is changing as a result of the running debate.

Madaus points to a few of the ideas emerging. He concurs with most teachers who see the genuine value of tests as diagnostic. Teachers want tests that identify the type of trouble learners are having and if possible the source. Certainly testing is appropriate for bilingual children or those with handicaps or disabilities. "We need tests," says Madaus, "that tell us why students are having trouble with such things as arithmetic algorithms or sequential comprehension. We don't have many of these genuinely diagnostic tests."[18] But he questions the use of so much mass testing. To probe how a school or a system is doing he would like to see more sampling—not only with standardized tests but sampling of students' knowledge in performing activities in which they demonstrate the ability to put knowledge and skills to use.

There is growing support for evaluation techniques that get beyond the narrow focus of paper and pencil tests. One such move with wide support by educators is a proposal by New York state's educational commissioner, Thomas Sobol, that the state's public schools rely less on standardized testing and more on broad measures like portfolios of students' work or individual projects. As Linda Darling-Hammond, of Teachers College, Columbia University, has pointed out, student evaluation in our major competitor countries is carried out not by mass-scored standardized tests but by a diversity of assessments—essays, oral examinations, practical performances (for example, conducting a scientific experiment), and student portfolios that shape a student's learning over time. In England, graduates submit such portfolios and take examinations in three of their chosen areas of specialty. In France, senior-level students take written and oral examinations in five areas, including philosophy, with probing questions like "Why should we defend the weak?" In Germany, assessment includes written exhibitions and oral examinations in science, mathematics, social studies, German, and a foreign language, as well as teacher recommendations and grades.[19]

The style and content of such assessments are a far cry from American students busily selecting "correct responses" on multiple-question sheet or selecting the right "solution" to pat questions or "problems." In the European models, assessment is not sharply demarcated from instruction but is done by teachers who examine their own students as well as those in other schools. In examining their own students, they get feedback on their teaching as well as their students' learning. Thus assessment can become a part of efforts at professional improvement, rather than a contest merely to compare and rank-order students, teachers, and schools.

Max Weber said bureaucracy is being perfected to the extent that it is dehumanized; that is, it can be refined by rules and procedures to handle every eventuality. If you view school learning as a production function, you can crack the whip over teachers and tighten prescriptions—refine expert-designed curriculum content, basals, work assignments, and tests. Perhaps you could upgrade all of this with computer technology in statewide or nationwide mainframes that would assure uniform coverage and provide electronic feedback on scores to central control stations. You could tighten surveillance and control—that is, automate. You could make Jeremy Bentham's dream come true: perfect control from the central tower.

When bureaucracy is conceived from a mechanistic metaphor, it is fatally flawed in that it fails to tap the human capacities for flexible creative responses. Bureaucratic functioning may make sense if we build in the rule that organizations must accommodate the distinctive "socio" dimensions of sociotechnical organization. That means the capacities for communication, dialogue, creative responses to problematic situations. The European models of assessment that give information feedback to teachers and students may be seen as encouraging an informating response. The American standardized testing model fails the test. To ensure creative teaching and evaluation, we must reject the command and control obsession for centralized test accountability. Once that difficult task is accomplished, we can invite a broad range of evaluation and testing procedures that our teachers believe in.

Madaus hopes that we will lower the stakes on testing "so that whatever we develop doesn't become corrupted in the way we have corrupted the kinds of instruments we're now using."[20] One fruitful avenue as we move deeper into the computer era is to use technology in which the line between instruction and evaluation is blurred. If teachers and students could get more immediate feedback at the learning site itself, they could learn from the nature of their mistakes and design remedial efforts. Once again this strategy, as In the Age of the Smart Machine, is to informate.

Resisting the Current Test Mania

It is instructive to listen to the ideas of teachers from southern Ohio whose central commitment is to make the style of learning in their schools consistent with the values of a democratic society. They think this central commitment is threatened by "the mad rush to embrace test scores as an all-inclusive evaluation of what goes on in schools." These teachers have used the fall 1990 issue of Democracy and Education at Ohio University to express their anger at how "the current test mania" destroys the values that give meaning and fulfillment to their work. They claim that their ideas about teaching are being stolen from them by the tests. They resent being bound by a curriculum built around short-term memorization of isolated facts. Moreover, they say their expertise is compromised by being forced to teach for the test: "Given materials programmed for the test, precise instruction on how to teach for the test, and the test itself, the teacher can be gradually pushed into the position of an assembly-line worker—making someone else's product, at someone else's speed, in someone else's manner."[21] Beyond that, test-driven teaching undermines their most valued goal: "to help students become cooperative, insightful, engaged, and reflective democratic citizens. . . . Overreliance on standardized testing seems to have the potential of making teaching for democracy nearly impossible. Such tests rely on competition, individual action, a belief that knowledge is static, and a focus on memorization and recitation. Teaching for democracy relies upon cooperation, group action, a belief that knowledge is fluid."[22]

Teachers like these tend to see evaluation and teaching as the same, not separate. As students and teachers work together, they try various forms of feedback to see if the learning has been integrated. This is very different from the standard question: How do our students compare against national norms? This question may be of passing interest, but to make it the central concern can vitiate the essence of teaching. It is time to ask for accountability from those who would exact such costs from teachers like these.

Such teachers do not ignore the widespread concern for evaluation. They are as interested in evaluation as anyone, but they want it in a form that is consistent with their goals. The National Center for Fair and Open Testing calls for "authentic evaluation." By this it means evaluation that directly measures actual performance in the subject. Authentic evaluation, also referred to as "performance," "appropriate," or "direct" evaluation, includes a wide variety of techniques: portfolios of work, teacher observations, checklists and inventories, exhibitions, written compositions, and more.

The portfolio technique, originally developed in the world of art as a sort of résumé, is being adopted in a variety of settings. In education, the word "portfolio" signifies the compilation of a student's work for review and assessment according to stated guidelines. The approach accomplishes two purposes: to document a record of major tasks accomplished and to evaluate the work in terms of established criteria. The California Mathematics Portfolio Guidelines, for example, specify that portfolios should contain samples of typical work (as judged by the teacher) and several "best efforts" (as decided jointly by the student and the teacher). The portfolio is to include two pieces of work on challenging mathematics problems from the beginning of the course and two from the end; one or two examples of imaginative or reflective work; one or two examples revealing evidence of persistence; and one piece representing the student's work in a small-group investigation.

For an example of a history exhibit, one can turn to Project Zero of Harvard's Graduate School of Education. After a unit on the Civil War, the teacher provides the class with a facsimile of letters written by recently freed slaves and the people who shaped Reconstruction. The task for an individual or a group is to study the letters, make notes, and design a museum exhibition that centers on the letters. The aim is to convey an understanding of the complexity of the postbellum South. Criteria for assessment include the ability to break out of stereotypes, work from original documents, furnish explanations for each item, and make or provide photocopies of other relevant artifacts.

One oral history project asks students to select a subject to interview, to develop a hypothesis based on early investigations, and to pose at least four questions to ask the interviewee in order to test the hypothesis. The evaluation assesses whether the questions are leading or biased, whether the student can discriminate between fact and opinion, and whether the student does follow-up investigations to check out the answers when possible. The organization of the final report, both written and audiotaped, is also judged.

Writing and reading can be assessed by means of authentic evaluation, as well. The National Assessment of Education Progress (NAEP) is developing materials in which students are asked to write on assigned topics. Their work is then graded by teams of readers, from the same or other schools, according to standard guidelines. The reading of young students may be evaluated best by having a student read aloud from materials of different levels of difficulty. The reading can be taped and reviewed by the teacher and student to identify strengths and weaknesses. In Upper Arlington, Ohio, assessment of reading at the K–3 level is done according to "Holistic Scoring Scales." A top level of 4 is given when a student reaches out to challenging books, appreciates humor, reads widely, remembers books, characters, and settings, summarizes and interprets a story effectively, and raises unique questions. Such assessments can be designed to follow the curriculum closely. They provide continuous information for teachers, and students can learn to assume responsibility for their portfolios and records and thereby become involved in regular self-analysis of their work.

The National Center for Fair and Open Testing argues that all forms of authentic testing can be summarized numerically or put on a scale to provide a variety of information about aggregate performance at the classroom, school, district, state, and national levels. Even so, there is no doubt that these broader forms of assessment can be misused if they are turned into just another version of test score comparison and categorizing. Improved assessment, no matter how well crafted, is not a panacea that will bring authentic reform to education.

These new techniques are less routinized and more complex than standard testing. They are not problem free, however, and require the energy of committed teachers. Communities who respond to such ideas are showing their respect for creative teachers as well as the community's concern for evidence of results. These developments represent a response to the clash of competing values noted at the beginning of this chapter: the right to know if children are learning versus the need to resist forms of testing that vitiate creative learning and integrity in teaching. The continuing question is whether we can design schooling that encompasses both values. If we cannot get a definitive answer, to which will we give priority?

In the newer alternatives to hierarchical prescription in both work and school, there is a tendency to place more control and trust in those at the work site itself, the workers and teachers, in order to tap their creative ideas about how to improve the quality of the effort. Having said this, we should never forget the significant differences between industrial production and the learning of children. Those Ohio teachers were interested in the democratic ideals not merely for the functional end of improving performance, but for their value in affecting the life and character of their students. They wanted to help their students become "cooperative, insightful, engaged, and reflective" because these qualities are the ones necessary to support personal growth in learning and because they are the qualities citizens need to support democratic community as a way of living.[23]

Number One by the Year 2000?

A major issue regarding testing and assessment will be posed by the six national goals for education for the year 2000 that were set by the governors and President Bush in February 1990. Consider just two of these goals:

- "Goal 3: By the year 2000, American students will leave grades 4, 8, and 12 having demonstrated competency in challenging subject matter including English, science, history, and geography; and every school in America will ensure that all students learn to use their minds well, so that they may be prepared for responsible citizenship, further learning, and productive employment."[24]
- "Goal 4: By the year 2000, U.S. students will be first in mathematics and science achievement."[25]

The pressures will be enormous to treat these goals as a horse race with the familiar standardized tests as the instruments for measurement and comparison.

Evidence of the pressure is found in the statement of John Ashcroft, Republican governor of Missouri and 1991–1992 chairman of the National Governors' Association. In August 1991, as he was to begin his term as chair, Ashcroft said that his plan was to set up action groups to shift the governors' focus to education. He thought this was a propitious time because business leaders across the country were getting involved in education. Educational leaders could learn from business how to streamline bureaucracies and ensure quality control. "Businesses," he said, "have learned the wastefulness of having an inspector at the end of the assembly line throwing defective products into a trash bin. Instead, manufacturing needs to be supervised all along the line. Likewise students needed to be tested throughout their school years." When told that many teachers feared that an increase in testing could restrict their flexibility and creativity, Ashcroft replied: "Testing doesn't interfere with teaching. All we want to do is measure progress. If learning increases we'll give teachers flexibility. We aren't going to allow teachers to pretend progress."[26]

Here we have the familiar argument. Standardized test scores are to be viewed as *the* measure of effective teaching. Test scores will go up if teachers are forced to work harder to get scores up. It is a no-nonsense way of "knowing" what the learning of children is about—and how to get improvement. Frustration with low national scores is understandable. When we do not really understand the complex factors involved, the temptation is strong to seize on a simplistic remedy that tells teachers how to get results: "Work harder. Teach them. Test them to show us you've taught them. And it won't cost more money." Such a formula may be irresistible.

But the complexities that Governor Ashcroft chose to ignore will not go away. We know, for example, the result of the previous fifteen years' effort to "achieve excellence" by the spur of testing: Scores finally stabilized or improved a bit—but at the expense of the higher-order thinking skills now most needed by our children. Furthermore, in the same month that Governor Ashcroft became head of the National Governors' Association, his commissioner of education in Missouri, Robert Bartman, reported interesting evidence about the test score problem that the governor did not address. Bartman said that we can see "an absolutely straight down-the-line correlation" between family incomes and college entrance exam scores on the Scholastic Aptitude Test (SAT). On the verbal portion of the SAT, 116 points separated students with family incomes of less than $10,000 from those of families of incomes of $70,000 or higher. On the mathematics portion of the SAT, 113 points separated the poor from the wealthy. And the gradations of scores in between correlated neatly with income.

Noting this trend, Donald M. Stewart, president of the College Board, which sponsors the SAT, expressed a concern that the nation was becoming "divided between a small class of an educational elite and an underclass of students academically ill-prepared for the demands of college or the workplace." It is not insignificant that the rich districts in Missouri spend nearly $6,000 more per pupil each year than do the poorest districts. In Illinois the corresponding figure is $10,000.[27] As the income gap between the upper two-fifths and the lower two-fifths of Americans has widened in the 1980s and early 1990s, we should not be surprised at disappointing results on national averages.

We will know when American leaders of government and business are ready to make a serious effort at improvement in scores: when they drop the single-minded obsession with *testing as the answer* and turn directly to the core issue of how to raise the family incomes of the growing number of the poor and the near poor. If we choose to ignore the poverty and violence that blight the lives of poor children, or fail to correct the inequities between poor and wealthy school districts, at least we could stop pontificating about being Number One in the world educationally by the year 2000. It is not going to happen.

Theoretically, we could resist the simplistic solution that kills enthusiasm for real learning. We could acknowledge the need to take on the hard task, barely begun, of assessing whether our children are learning by means appropriate to the goals of higher-order learning and essential skills. We could listen to creative, caring teachers to see if we trust their methods. We could be willing to learn with them while more authentic assessment techniques are invented and refined. We could acknowledge that this path will require us to take on the challenging task of restructuring American schools. As Linda Darling-Hammond put it in "Achieving Our Goals: Superficial or Structural Reforms?":

> The key question for the national goals movement, then, is whether our policy makers will roll up their sleeves *and tackle the structural issues that underlie the problems of American schools,* or whether they will think they have solved the problems by setting standards and giving more tests to see if they have been met. If they believe that standards setting [and testing] is the solution rather than merely a way of framing the problem, then we will lose perhaps our last chance to create a model for 21st century schools that can offer more than rhetoric on the subjects of educational excellence and equality.[28]

Resolving the Tension

We face a complex problem: The call for evaluation and evidence of accomplishment is legitimate. Despite all my criticisms of testing, I acknowledge that testing has a significant role to play. Life itself tests us. There are performance levels that must be met before we may be trusted with important work roles in society. We sometimes need to be tested to discover our limits, to identify our weaknesses and our strengths. And educators need feedback on their efforts in order to determine their successes and deficiencies. At the same time, we have to work from the truth: Testing can be misused and we can deceive ourselves into thinking its numbers tell us more than, in fact, they do. If testing damages the integrity of teaching and learning, it is self-defeating. We are confronted then with this tension between two values: the need to know results (ascertained in a variety of ways including a repertoire of tests) versus the need to protect the integrity of learning and teaching. The legitimate task is to seek creative resolutions of this tension.

One approach would be to ask teachers—those with a demonstrated record of success with students, including those from blighted neighborhoods—what method of assessment helps or hinders them? And as an educational policymaker I would listen to them. We want to help them continue their good results. One such person is Deborah Meier, who has gained national praise as founder and director of the Central Park East public schools in New York City. When asked what she thought about standardized reading tests, she replied:

> Standardized reading tests measure a variety of things, but reading is not among them. Students are given a sentence with one word missing, and they're asked to supply the word. Or they're given a paragraph, completely out of any context, and asked questions about that paragraph. Some students do well at such tests and some don't; there may or may not be a correlation between these results and students' ability to read. These test results certainly don't necessarily correspond with people who find the written word powerful, important, interesting, and accessible.
>
> But that's not the biggest problem with these tests. To focus on, say, ability to answer multiple-choice questions as a *definition* of reading means that schools come to focus on it as a *method* of reading. Schools with children who tend to do well on these tests also expose the kids to real books; then maybe they also spend a day or two giving test practice. But schools with student bodies that don't have as much exposure to literacy at home, whose students tend to score lower on such tests, aim exclusively at preparing kids for the tests. It's precisely these children who most need to learn that the written word can have real power. They're deprived of the opportunity

to experience that power in part because of this reductive definition of reading. So the problem isn't just that it's a bad definition but that its impact on education is precisely to further deprive the kids who most need to be introduced to the pleasures and rewards of reading.

A lot of the people who advocate national testing are calling for different kinds of assessment tools, which presumably would measure more important intellectual habits—through the use of portfolios, essays, and so on. Although I would find such an effort considerably less objectionable, I think that trying to create these sophisticated tools, trying to develop a consensus about them, trying to figure out how to standardize them, will be extraordinarily difficult or even impossible—not to mention expensive—both to develop and implement. And in order to standardize the national exam, you would have to further standardize the curriculum. And that would be a mistake.

If you take the idea of choice seriously, I think you end up looking toward different kinds of assessments—assessments developed at the level of the school. When we worked out our own standards of assessment at our school, it required a great deal of discussion and a great deal of time, but the time wasn't wasted, because through these discussions we were creating an educational community. It was a form of R&D, and a form of staff development. We were creating our own methods and values, thinking them through. And if some of our students disagree with our standards, they can argue about it with us, and we can either defend the standards or modify them after hearing them out. It's not something that was developed somewhere else, and that we're stuck with. If you're trying to persuade kids

about the power of human reasoning, then it's
important that the standards by which they're
judged be accessible to their own reason, and
open to their appeal. They need to accept responsibility for their education and thus to "own" the
tools by which they're measured.[29]

Deborah Meier and her teachers at Central Park East
have demonstrated their effectiveness with inner-city children—including impressive test score results. If we listen, we
learn that teachers like these do not fear assessment. They
welcome the kind that coincides with their values and helps
them to get their children to be enthusiastic learners. They
resist mandated testing by bureaucratic centralist prescription
that not only interferes with their work but damages it.

The truth is that our strongest source of hope lies in
American creativity. It exists among American teachers, and
among those imaginative, energetic people who would choose
teaching if the nature of the work warranted it. We need to
keep listening to what these creative ones tell us about what
hinders or helps them to work with integrity. We cannot get
what we need without it.

Eight

Restructuring:
New Strategies for Learning

The traditional model of classroom organization, as well as that of the school system, creates . . . problems that adversely affect or greatly constrict the productivity of all participants in the educational arena. What we have now is not working to anyone's satisfaction.
—Seymour Sarason (1990)

By the end of the 1980s, as we have seen, misgivings about top-down, test score accountability were growing. There was mounting awareness that efforts at coercive reform had left us with huge problems: alarming numbers of school dropouts, inadequate learning by unengaged students, and low morale among the teachers. Moreover, the anxiety was sharpened by the sense of America's vulnerability in the world market. The focus on learning as mastery of basic skills with success for only some students was simply not tolerable. That model was dysfunctional: It had failed to produce committed young Americans capable of the creativity and flexibility demanded by the problems of work-world change and social and ecological damage. As we entered the 1990s a call began to emerge for a new wave of reform—for a fundamental restructuring of schools in both management style and styles of teaching and learning. This chapter reports on examples of these early restructuring efforts.

What Is Restructuring?

An important impetus for "restructuring" came from the 1988 report of the Carnegie Foundation for the Advancement of Learning, "An Imperiled Generation/Saving Urban Schools," which announced that teachers have too little control over their work in schools with respect to selection of books and materials, course content, and the use of classroom time. As we have seen, in 1989, President Bush's new secretary of education, Lauro Cavazos, declared that after the failure of top-down reform we could not hope for real educational improvement while leaving the basic structure of the schools untouched. The call for restructuring triggered such a wide response that the American Association of School Administrators commissioned a book by Anne Lewis, *Restructuring America's Schools* (1989), to inform its members what this second wave of reform was all about.

As restructuring quickly became yet another amorphous reform concept, an attempt at definition was necessary. It came to include everything from ideas for local school autonomy to proposals for better teacher salary scales. Anne Lewis, who found more than forty major ideas connected with the concept, gave school administrators a useful summary of central themes by referring to comments by leading advocates of restructuring. Jane David, for example, a consultant to the Center for Policy Research on Education, offered a one-sentence summary: "The goal of restructuring is long-term comprehensive change guided by a conception of schools as stimulating workplaces and learning environments."[1]

Frank Newman, president of the Education Commission of the States, maintained that the key was to restructure so that students could become active learners—partners in the learning process. To do that would require leadership that would empower teachers in decision making.

A RAND report, *Steady Work*, said that a shift was needed away from mandating structures, rules, and resource allocations to giving people who work in schools the power to develop workable solutions with opportunities to fail and "the time to succeed."

Restructuring is different, said Albert Shanker, president of the American Federation of Teachers, in that "it seeks to create new relationships for children and teachers." Another union leader said that restructuring is concerned with the dynamics of learning, especially collaboration and problem solving.

David Florio of the National Science Foundation argued that the goal of restructuring is to open up learning, human interaction, and decision making. To help students get higher levels of success in learning, he said, we need schools with structures flexible enough to accommodate different interests, rates of learning, and content.

Ernest Boyer, president of the Carnegie Foundation for the Advancement of Teaching, stressed the theme of school-based management and local school autonomy. Mary Anne Raywid of Hofstra University articulated the case for public schools of choice. Theodore Sizer, founder of the Coalition of Essential Schools, offered a succinct summary: The goal of restructured schools is "to teach students to think."

There were observations, too, from those concerned with how to help American industry become competitive. Sue Berryman, director of the Institute on Education and the Economy at Teachers College, Columbia University, explained that because of the volatility of jobs, young people need to know how to learn. She pointed to what we already have noted: In mass production, workers are attached to isolated tasks; in reorganized work, job responsibilities are broadened and intermeshed, requiring teamwork. With flatter hierarchies, quality control and supervision are assigned to workers with the ability to self-regulate and, when necessary, to employ conflict resolution skills. The growing need, even for jobs considered low-skilled, is for higher-order thinking skills. Berryman pointed out that "when we recall how work has changed—the need to deal with uncertainty, to understand the firm's market environment, to understand the organizational context in which one's job is embedded, to anticipate, to deal with the unfamiliar and with discontinuity—we see a stunning parallel between these changes in the nature and structure of work and the defining characteristics of higher-order thinking."[2]

From the corporate world itself came observations by Owen Butler, former chairman of Procter & Gamble and chair of the Committee for Economic Development: "We are trying to change the way we go about educating our young. . . . We are trying to change from a system in which teachers are regarded as almost assembly-line classroom production workers to a system in which teachers are free to innovate and experiment and use creativity to improve teaching. We are trying to deregulate, to move the control of the schools from top-down to bottom-up. We are trying to provide better financing and attract better people into the profession. This requires a total change in 'corporate culture.' "[3]

This rhetoric reflects awareness of the need for the *informating* style of learning. But we should not fool ourselves into believing that a broad shift of this nature will come easily. As we entered the 1990s, two competing forces were at work. One was a growing recognition of the need for a fundamental reconceptualizing and restructuring of schooling. The other was cultural resistance to change based on long-seated American habits: a deep distrust of proposals to change schools as we have known them and a preference for a horse-race style of competition that would enable easy identification of winners and losers.

Before turning to examples of significant restructuring, let us first note some sources of resistance. There is, for example, the firm commitment of perhaps most Americans to "real schools" with kids at their desks in rows: listening to the teacher up front, studying the basal texts, filling out the worksheets, taking the tests. This model did produce learning that enabled many to get on in industrial America. It is the pattern that John Goodlad, in *Study of Schooling,* called "the deep structure of schooling" that has not changed much since 1900. It emerged with the rapid expansion of the public school system and the construction of "egg-crate" buildings designed to contain large numbers of squirming urban children. A major motivation was control—control of students, teachers, and instruction under conditions of mass education. It was a fitting counterpart to the factory modes of production that were controlling the labor of the adults. The structure became nearly impervious to the waves of reform that periodically broke against it. Supported by tradition, backed by vested administrative interests, it became the conventional wisdom in communities with parents who wanted "real school" for their kids: the same kind they themselves had had.

At the same time, by the opening of the 1980s, there was a growing sense that the complex problems of the onrushing postindustrial society could not be accommodated by time-honored formats. There was diminishing confidence, for example, that the agonizing problems of urban schooling could be solved by the model educator put forward by Secretary Bennett: the New Jersey principal, Joe Clark, with his bullhorn and baseball bat.

The plea for restructuring is a large order, but serious efforts beyond the rhetoric were being made—from system-wide efforts to those in local schools. We settle here for some examples that illustrate the range of changes that were emerging as we entered the 1990s. Mary Anne Raywid, a close student of restructuring reform, says that if one cuts through the complexity and ambiguity two broad strategies have emerged: site-based management and schools of choice.[4]

Site-Based Management

Dade County, Florida, under the leadership of Joseph Fernandez, did creative pioneering with school-based management. The general move has been to provide more autonomy for each school with significant teacher involvement in decision making.[5]

Dade County (Miami) reflects the changes and challenges of a major metro area in flux: a constant inflow of new students, many of whom do not speak English, racial tension, overcrowding, inadequate funding, and more. But there was a saving feature: Its superintendent and school board had full confidence that good teachers, with good environments for working, contained the key to improved education. There was a long-standing cooperative relationship between the teachers' union and management.

In 1987, a joint management/union team, following recommendations of the Carnegie Forum's Task Force on Teaching as a Profession, selected thirty-three schools from fifty-five applicants to participate in school-based management. The general aim was to get better education by "empowering schools to be more responsive and adaptive to change." Some of the features include:

- Participating schools have been given flexible control over 90 percent of their budgets (compared to about 10 percent for other schools).
- Each school may set up whatever governing structure it wants as long as there is ample room for teacher participation. Many schools have introduced Quality Circles to learn to implement cooperative planning (which is not easy after years of following directives). As changes emerge from the bottom, the administrative structure of the whole district has flattened. Schools can now develop their own plans for peer evaluation of teachers or principals.
- Each school receives more than $6,000 for staff development with time provisions for school improvement conferences for teachers and principals.
- Schools can request waivers of district or state regulations through a special committee set up for implementation— for example, to hire noncertified teachers with special talents.

Gerald Dreyfuss, assistant superintendent and director of the project, acknowledges that the most difficult part has been for people to learn to work and solve problems cooperatively. One of the major gains has been to see the reversal of white flight by middle-class parents as they sense a new vitality in the public schools.

With his success in Dade County, Superintendent Joseph Fernandez was invited to become the administrative head of schools in New York City. There he quickly moved to introduce an agreement with the union for a "school-based option." It allows schools to restructure when 75 percent of the teachers and the principal agree on a plan to better the learning/working environment for students and teachers. With less consistent support in New York, he is encountering resistance from school administrators there.

Schools of Choice

One of the best examples of the "schools of choice" strategy mentioned by Raywid is the work being done in Manhattan's District 4 in New York City. It combines the theme of local school autonomy with another idea for freeing teachers and principals from bureaucratic regulation: the idea of allowing parents to choose the school their child will attend. Accountability to the central board is replaced by accountability to parents.[6] Behind this concept is the idea that schools will reach for high quality by having to attract clientele. A related aim is to give teachers of individual schools a chance to design their own educational program so that they may present parents with unique choices. Each school is seen as an independent agent responsible to its clientele.

East Harlem was a fascinating place to try such an idea because Community School District 4 was probably the most impoverished of the city's thirty-two community school districts. Critics have argued that choice will only work with middle or upper-income parents who are sophisticated enough to take advantage of choices. District 4 was a perfect setting to test that hypothesis. Poverty and despair are endemic among East Harlem's 113,000 residents: 35 percent receive public assistance; the median household income of $8,300 is the lowest of Manhattan's communities; over 50 percent of families are headed by single females; more than 20 percent of the building lots are vacant or occupied by abandoned buildings. Some 60 percent of the students are Hispanic (10 percent classified as "limited English proficient"), 35 percent African American, 4 percent white, 1 percent Asian. Before the implementation of the program, District 4 ranked thirty-second in reading achievement scores among the 32 community school districts.

District 4 developed the features of its alternative program slowly over a ten-year period. One of its unique features is that it has forty-four schools in twenty buildings. Thus a school is not equivalent to a building: A school is an *educational program* organized around a central theme and headed by a director or a principal. In some instances the school director is a teacher. At the elementary level, there are five alternative schools—each has a unique theme and accepts applicants from any interested parents. The twenty-four junior high schools all accept enrollees from anywhere in the district. Some are organized around themes while others are run as traditional schools.

The designers all stress the importance of taking time to develop sound programs. A full-choice junior high program was not offered until eight years after the project began. Each school was given up to a year to plan its offering; only three to five schools were opened in one year. The "small is beautiful" principle was followed: no more than four classes at each grade level. The designers also emphasize a feeling of ownership. Students and parents feel ownership because they choose the schools; teachers and directors feel ownership because they develop the concept and plans.

In applying for a school, parents are given an information booklet describing the school's range of offerings. They visit the schools of choice and ask the staff about the learning style and workload expected. Students may make up to six choices with a written explanation for each. Most schools require personal interviews. The staff of each school retains control over the selection process with the proviso that no more than 20 percent of its students may come from outside District 4. In effect, a social contract is established between each school and each family: "This is the kind of school we are. If you choose us, you choose to work within our guidelines."

The range of diversity is indicated by some of the themes in the junior high schools: Health and Biomedical Studies, Computer Science, Performing Arts, Career Academy, Human Services School, Maritime School, BETA (for those who have had trouble adjusting to traditional schools), Bridge School (with an atmosphere similar to that of private prep schools), Central Park Community East (a charter member of Ted Sizer's Coalition of Essential Schools), Bilingual School, Science and Humanities.

Ten years of operation have produced some striking results. Whereas at the beginning only 15 percent of students could read above grade level, by 1988 the proportion was 63 percent. In 1983, District 4 ranked twenty-third in mathematics achievement; by 1988 it ranked nineteenth. In placement in New York's highly selective high schools such as Stuyvesant Bronx Science, Brooklyn Tech, and La Guardia School of Music and the Performing Arts, fewer than ten District 4 students had been admitted in the mid 1970s, while 139 were admitted in 1987.

District 4 also redesigned the ailing Franklin High School, where daily attendance had hovered around 45 percent. The new high school became the Manhattan Center for Science and Mathematics. Nearly 87 percent of the students who entered it in 1982 had earned a diploma by 1988—compared with a citywide average of 54 percent. Although the school is now independent of the district, it shows that school redesign growing out of the choice policy can lead to high-quality education in a desperate urban poverty area. The human desire for something better is there. It shows what can happen when a democratic framework is created that can tap the innovative but disciplined commitment of adults and children.

The president's Education Summit with the governors in September 1989 gave new impetus to a bewildering array of proposals for restructuring. Statewide plans arose from Maine to California. Additional big-city systems, where poverty-induced problems were acute, began to respond. The most dramatic of these was in Chicago, whose schools had been labeled by the voluble Secretary Bennett as the worst in the nation. A quick glance may be in order to indicate why a turn to democratic styles was deemed necessary. Bennett had told a national audience that Chicago's schools were "close to educational meltdown"—and in this case there was evidence to support him. About 50 percent of the students were dropping out. Reading scores in nearly half the schools were in the bottom 1 percent of the nation. On college entrance exams, the city's high schools had fifty-nine of the sixty-one lowest average scores in the Chicago metropolitan area.[7]

Gradually the perception had arisen that the dug-in rigidity of a swollen school bureaucracy was a major impediment to improvement—and that its adversary, the Chicago Teachers Union, had equally alienated parents and the community. The drastic situation finally called forth a drastic response. Under the leadership of a research advocacy group, Designs for Change, a coalition of forty business, community, and parent organizations, the Alliance for Better Chicago Schools was formed. It resulted in securing passage of a school reform measure by the Illinois State Legislature in July 1988.

The School Reform Act contained one of the most radical restructuring plans in the country. Each public school is now governed by an elected council consisting of eight parents and community residents, two teachers, and the principal. The council hires the principal under a four-year contract, allocates budgetary resources, and frames long-term plans for school improvement. Principals hire staff from certified applicants, and a teacher with an unsatisfactory rating can be fired after a 45-day probationary period. Teacher advisory committees are created to help the local school council and principal shape school improvement plans. Each school council elects a representative to a district council that will select the district superintendent and monitor local schools. A new Chicago-wide school board was appointed by the mayor from candidates screened by a citizens nominating committee. The central district budget was cut by $40 million, and these funds are passed on to the local school. An Oversight Authority was established by the mayor and governor for five years to see that school administrators carry out the plan.

This bold plan to place the public schools of a huge American city—one with manifold financial, racial, and social class problems—under democratic decentralized control faces daunting challenges in the grinding political/social tensions of the Windy City. In a system this huge, there are bound to be mixed results. Nonetheless, one can cite examples of several positive developments.

Significant changes have been made in a large high school in a Puerto Rican neighborhood. Active parent involvement on the local school council has led to enriched programs of Puerto Rican cultural awareness not only for students but also for teachers, many of whom are Anglos. Children are learning of the beauty of the island and the cultural accomplishments of its people. They are studying the island's history from a Puerto Rican perspective. The committee is also initiating a broad range of community services that make use of the building beyond the regular school hours.

In a preschool program, accomplished teachers are designated as mentors or lead teachers. Their task is to train other teachers, and they have developed a collaborative program of supervision by fellow teachers. Teachers are being energized by having *their* ideas listened to.

No matter what the result, the Chicago plan is bound to be a major learning experience for metropolitan America.

Local Restructuring for Minorities

While these systemwide efforts are significant, we should not be deluded into thinking they are typical of what is going on in American schools in general. A 1990 MIT study on minority education estimates that probably no more than 1 to 2 percent of American schools are involved in some kind of restructuring. For a movement that has as a guiding principle the concept of decentralizing, we need to look at some of the

host of local examples. We focus here on programs relating
to one of America's most serious problems: the education of
minorities.

One of the most comprehensive reports on schooling
for minorities was the Massachusetts Institute of Technology's
Education That Works (1990),[8] an outcome of the Quality
Education for Minorities Project that brought together the
thinking of prominent minority and nonminority educators.
(Included were representatives of Native Americans, African
Americans, Puerto Ricans, and Mexican Americans.) The
MIT report came out unequivocally for restructuring, saying
that the education of minority youth cannot be improved
"without radical restructuring of our schools."[9] The writers
of the report were well aware that less than 20 percent of new
entrants into the work force by the year 2000 will be white
males, and that the public schools as presently organized are
failing to educate a large percentage of minority children for
the electronic-era society.

It is the factory model of schooling, they report, which
is cheating minority students. They say the reforms of the
early 1980s merely reinforced the factory school's weaknesses—reinforcing it by the simple call for "the basics," by
imposing prescriptions from above, and by making teachers
and students accountable to standardized test scores:

> Factory schools teach students to memorize
> through drill and practice rather than through
> the use of knowledge and skills to solve problems,
> innovate, and learn. The factory model treats stu-
> dents as objects to be acted on rather than as
> active participants in their own learning. The
> factory model assumes that teachers need not
> have the higher-order thinking skills because
> they, like factory workers, only need to follow the
> rules imposed from above. Above all the factory
> model ignores individual differences by assuming
> that there is one best way to learn and teach. It
> assumes that management's responsibility is to

> understand what is best for the system and im-
> pose it through bureaucracies on teachers and
> students. . . . The factory model measures every-
> thing and rewards nothing. . . . [It] assumes as
> true what is known to be false, namely that intel-
> ligence and achievement are standardized and
> therefore measurable by objective tests.[10]

Furthermore, the report says the factory model is repelling many able teachers by its "stultifying, even degrading, working environments, by poor outcomes for most students, and by low pay and professional status."[11]

It is no wonder, then, as Mary Anne Raywid put it, that "minority students hate school . . . so that if we want to keep 'at risk' youngsters in school we are going to have to provide a different kind of school environment . . . with a different kind of organizational structure and a different feel and flavor."[12] The authors of the MIT report endorse this position by asking for a restructuring—one that relies more heavily on participative processes at the point of learning and recognizes differences in individual experiences, knowledge, and learning and teaching styles. Such a restructured school would give teachers and the principal the power to implement their own ideas. It would encourage risk taking in order to secure better learning results.

The MIT report points to James Comer's work in New Haven, Connecticut, as a demonstration of effective restructuring.[13] Starting in 1968, Comer and his colleagues at the Yale Child Study Center developed a model that greatly improved the performance of two of New Haven's thirty-three schools with the lowest achievement and worst attendance records. Some 99 percent of children in the two schools were black, and 70 percent of the families were on welfare. By 1983, fifteen years later, the two schools—with the same socioeconomic composition—ranked third and fifth in composite fourth-grade test scores and had superior attendance records. There had been no serious behavior problems in more than a decade.

Comer had created processes and structures that changed attitudes, incentives, and behavior. He established a basic participatory management plan in which the principals shared power with parents, teachers, and support staff. Teachers paid attention to child development concepts, and everyone involved accepted Comer's conviction that these children, with hard work and good attitudes, could learn as well as anyone. Comer and his colleagues recognized that major changes had to come from within the school itself, since in this inner-city community many of the basic institutions—religious, economic, and social—were ailing and in trouble. Governance and management teams were created with parents, teachers, mental health specialists, and support staff elected as members. They decided to concentrate on problem solving by consensus rather than formal voting. This policy facilitated joint discussions and eased communication between parents and the professional staff. They agreed to seek professional help for dealing with student behavioral problems they were not trained to address. By giving each member a sense of participation in the decisions, the consensus style avoided feelings of division into winners and losers.

Comer's model, with its self-correcting process of development, became the School Development Program and has spread to more than fifty other schools. Ultimately, Comer became convinced that the key ingredients were the governance team, the mental health group, and parental involvement. Out of the process came the central conviction: "With each intervention the [school] staff became increasingly sensitive to the concerns of developing children and to the fact that behavior problems result mainly from unmet needs rather than from willful badness—and that actions can be taken to meet these needs."[14]

Comer's School Development Program and Harlem's District 4 demonstrate that ideas from the restructuring movement can tap the learning potential of impoverished children in ways the factory model fails to do. That is encouraging. But all of the children and adults involved are under constant threat from the shameful poverty and violence that surround the schools. One response—that of Harlem's P.S. 208—is to turn the school into a community center, open in the late afternoon for children of working parents and open in the evening for parent education and community events. As a community center, the community school can coordinate the social, health, and vocational services that the children and their families need.

The Accelerated Schools Project

An imaginative, promising program emerged at the end of the 1980s: the Accelerated Schools Project initiated by Henry Levin and colleagues at Stanford University. It is appropriate to end with this program because it was designed as a direct response to one of our most urgent problems: how to tap the latent learning capacities of the huge number of America's "at-risk" or "disadvantaged" children so that they can become effective participants in the emerging postindustrial economy.

Henry Levin was ideally prepared to take on this question. He is director of the Center for Educational Research at Stanford and has held joint appointments in the School of Education and the Department of Economics. He has done voluminous research on the relations between education and the economy, as illustrated by one of his many books, *Schooling and Work in the Democratic State* (1985, with Martin Carnoy).[15]

Who are America's at-risk students and how do they affect the economy? In Levin's program, they are described as children who lack the home and community resources to benefit fully from conventional school programs. They are concentrated among impoverished minority groups, immigrants, non-English-speaking families, and single-parent homes. They lack the experiences that lead to educational success— access to good nutrition and medical care, to early learning programs, and to educational interactions at home such as rich language experiences.

Standard efforts to relate to their deficiencies often consist of remedial or compensatory services that fail to be effective. When put in slow classes, these children and their teachers tend to be stigmatized. As expectations for them are lowered, they tend to fall farther behind their classmates. By assuming that the basics come first, emphasis is put on the mechanics of basic skills that fail to tap their interests and motivation. The little contact that the schools have with parents often consists of reports on the inadequacies and misconduct of their children.

The number of disadvantaged children is growing rapidly for several reasons. America is experiencing waves of immigrants, legal and illegal, from some of the poorest countries in Latin America and Asia—three-quarters of the world's immigrants enter the United States. Moreover, the parents of the poor tend to be younger and have higher birthrates. Finally, in the last fifteen years there has been a doubling of female-parent families and a 30 percent rise in the poverty rate among children.[16] Recent estimates suggest that about 30 percent of children in elementary and secondary schools are disadvantaged—with expectations of a continued rise in their numbers.[17]

While some of these children succeed in spite of the handicaps, the school experience for many is a sad failure. Because of poverty and language and cultural differences, they begin school without the skills and support necessary for success. They lag behind in school achievement in the elementary grades so that by the sixth grade they are about two years below grade level—by the twelfth grade, if they are still there, they are four years behind. It is no surprise that among American children they have the highest dropout rate. We have become familiar with the dismal statistics: One in eight 17-year-olds is illiterate; a U.S. government study reported that in 1971 the percentage of illiterates among Hispanics and African Americans was 56 percent and 44 percent respectively;[18] a 1972 study estimated that the loss of lifetime earnings for the group who failed to complete high school was about $237 billion.[19] The moral tragedy is compounded as these young Americans, before they leave their teens, have become obsolete for participating as worker-citizens in the competitive postindustrial economy.

The seriousness of the situation is penetrating the awareness of corporate executives as they feel the impact of a shortfall of qualified young people. Edward Franklin, president of Chevron Oil, a company that has now made a major commitment to the Accelerated Schools Project, says that Chevron is currently turning away 60 percent of young people applying for jobs in the San Francisco Bay area because they cannot read or do simple mathematics problems.[20]

By the end of the 1980s, Henry Levin, aware of the growing human and economic crisis (and aware too that a major financial response would not be made by our political leaders), came up with an alternative idea to present failed policies: the Accelerated Schools Project.[21] The basic ideas are not terribly complex. These children need *accelerated* learning because at-risk students must learn at a faster rate than their more privileged peers, not at a slower rate that leaves them further behind. To learn more effectively, they need the kind of enriched learning programs typically provided for gifted students, not a slowed-down remedial program. Instead of "drill and kill" worksheets, they need help from powerful instructional techniques and a curriculum relevant to their interests. The overall goal, an ambitious one, is to accelerate learning so that these at-risk children will be learning at grade level by the time they finish the sixth grade. As they proceed through the secondary grades, one should expect reduced dropouts, reduced drug use, and reduced pregnancies.

The Accelerated Schools Project is built on three basic principles: unity of purpose, empowerment, and building on strengths. *Unity of purpose* refers to an agreement by all partners in the school community—teachers, administrators, parents, and children—to be guided by a common set of goals: a common vision. The general goal is to help the children become academically able and, beyond that, to create specific, active goals for curriculum, instruction, and school climate that can guide daily practice.

Empowerment means giving power to key figures in the local school community, including parents, to make important educational decisions and take responsibility for the outcomes.

Having learned from Comer's school management teams, each accelerated school has an overall steering committee and task force composed of the principal, the teachers, other staff, and parents. Decisions are made at the local site about the choice of curriculum and instructional materials, the allocation of resources and personnel, and instructional strategies. When necessary, action is taken to get waivers of curriculum mandates or teachers' union regulations.

Building on strengths refers to using all of the resources that students, parents, teachers, administrators, and the community have to facilitate effective learning. Instead of hobbling teachers by frameworks that control them, they are encouraged to bring to their task their gifts of insight, intelligence, and idealism. Instead of seeing parents as obstacles, they are brought into the school's thinking and its activities. They help locate community resources—for example, senior citizens, youth programs, business and church groups. Finally, the "disadvantaged" children are viewed in terms of the unique assets they can bring to stimulating learning: diverse cultural traditions, capacities of oral and artistic expression, and the ability to help each other learn through peer tutoring and cooperative learning. Freed from their "command" roles in enforcing prescribed regulations, administrators have an opportunity to interact creatively with parents, teachers, children, and the surrounding community. Twice a month, at one of the schools, teachers swap roles with the principal.

Parents have a central role. It is assumed that they love their children, want them to succeed, and need to be brought into active participation. The Daniel Webster School of San Francisco, one of the first in the project, created a Parent Involvement Committee that arranged creation of a Parent Room, with coffee and comfortable furniture, where parents could meet as they arrived before or after school. Parents became involved as volunteers in the classroom, playground, and front office and became members of parent education classes. They took an active role in planning PTA and other school meetings, which began to attract large crowds.

A glimpse of the style of learning at Daniel Webster is provided in the second *Associated Schools Newsletter* (Spring 1991). Daniel Webster is situated in the Potrero district of San Francisco, marked by inner-city problems of drugs, gangs, and crime. Most of the children are on the free or reduced-fee breakfast and lunch program and represent an ethnic mix of African Americans, Hispanics, Native Americans, Chinese, Anglos, and other cultures.

The school follows a basic principle that is taken for granted in programs for the gifted—the idea that everyone needs wiggle room, which means that teachers, children, and parents need freedom to pursue knowledge in ways they find interesting. Thus the classrooms at the Webster School are filled with plants, animals, and student artwork and writing that grow out of the variety of ways children are learning. On one classroom wall is a poster showing the activities for which parents have volunteered. Some learning is organized around broad themes into which a variety of skills and subject matter can be integrated. A third-grade theme is Native American culture. The room is filled with student-made Indian artifacts, Indian crops children have grown, Indian craft products, and dioramas. A Chevron grant made it possible for the class to attend a Native American Pow-Wow at Stanford University with opportunities to see authentic Indian culture presented by various tribes. From interactions with the Indians, teachers and students developed new ideas for a Native American Museum to be created at the school. A fifth-grade class produces books that are on display at the local library. Two fifth-grade teachers secured a grant for a unit on "Our World, Our Environment" that will culminate in a trip to an ocean aquarium.

Throughout all of the school's activities there is one common objective: to create learning opportunities in a language-rich environment. In short, it is a school alive with learning—the kind of learning one finds in good schools with enriched programs in more favored communities. The primary purpose of the Daniel Webster School is to provide learning that is exciting, challenging, and engaging, but there has been a by-product. In 1990, the Daniel Webster Accelerated School showed the largest percentage gain on the California Test of Basic Skills in language and the second-largest gain in mathematics among all of the seventy San Francisco elementary schools.

While the total Accelerated Schools Project is too new to offer definitive evidence of results here, the reports coming in are generally positive. The newness of the program is shown by the fact that its first newsletter came out in the winter of 1991. Its appearance coincided with two important facts. First, the program had expanded from two pilot elementary schools in 1987–1988 to more than fifty elementary and middle schools by 1990–1991. (State networks were being established in Illinois and Missouri and satellite centers in Houston, Los Angeles, New Orleans, and San Francisco.) Second, another grant from Chevron U.S.A. had been added to an original $1.45 million grant awarded in 1989.[22]

Levin and colleagues wanted to demonstrate that significant improvements could be made in the learning of at-risk children—without major new financial investments—by restructuring thinking and the strategies for stimulating learning. They are demonstrating their point. At the same time, one cannot avoid comparing the vast resources of American corporations who want to be part of a world-class economy with the pitiful school resources that this same economy provides for its millions of disadvantaged children. Levin and colleagues estimate that an additional $21 billion of funding, beyond Chapter 1 money, would be required to *begin* to show what could be done with our forgotten children.[23]

Restructuring Society Itself

We need good ideas—exciting ideas like those of the Accelerated Schools Project. The truth is, however, that if they lack the funding and start with a "crash program psychology" without allowing time for everyone to absorb the values and spirit of the program, they can falter or fail. I know of such instances.

The diverse programs I have described are examples of ideas that emerged in the early 1990s in response to the need to restructure American schooling. They demonstrate that we do have the creative capacity to design learning appropriate for the new era. That is all to the good. But we should not lose sight of the fact that it is unrealistic and unfair to rely simply on "school fix" answers to the curse of poverty and shocking economic inequality that grew sharply in the 1980s. The democratic vision may help restructure the quality of life in our schools, but that vision mocks us until this country gets serious about a democratic restructuring of society at large. By shirking that daunting task, we are inhibiting our best efforts at educational and economic reform.

Harold Hodgkinson, director of the Center for Demographic Policy of the Institute for Educational Leadership, Washington, D.C., has assembled evidence showing why we are frustrated by the meager results issuing from the rash of reform efforts—by the negligible change in high school graduation rates, in most test scores, and in other indicators of quality.[24] To pinpoint the underlying problem, Hodgkinson uses a metaphor: "the house of American schooling wasted by an unrepaired leaking roof." The many well-intentioned efforts to patch the understructure are washed out by continuous damage from the unattended leaky roof.

The "leaky roof" is the dramatic change that has occurred in the condition of children coming to American schools since 1980. The grim fact is that about one-third of preschool children will experience failure in school "because of poverty, neglect, sickness, handicapping conditions, and lack of adult protection and nurturance."[25] A few examples from Hodgkinson's figures illustrate the point:

- One-fourth of all preschool American children since 1987 have been living in poverty (the highest rate of any industrialized nation).
- One-fourth of pregnant mothers receive no health care in the crucial first trimester of pregnancy.
- Every year about 350,000 babies are born to cocaine-

addicted mothers. These children later suffer from short attention span and poor coordination, among other problems.

- Two million school-age children have no supervision by adults after school, and another 2 million are being raised by neither parent.
- Reports of child abuse or neglect in 1987 were triple those of 1976 and the numbers are rising.[26]

Behind many facts like these are major changes taking place in American families. Only 6 percent follow the classic model of a working father, a homemaker mother, and two children. The U.S. divorce rate of about 50 percent is the highest in the world. Children living with one parent increased from 12 percent in 1970 to 25 percent in 1989. More than 50 percent of all white children and 75 percent of African American children are likely to live for some portion of their formative years with their mother only.[27] Fifteen million children are living with single mothers with family incomes that average about $11,400 (within $1,000 of the poverty level)—in comparison with an average income of $34,000 for a married couple with children.

With the best intentions in the world, children from poverty or near-poverty homes suffer disproportionately from health and nutrition problems, lack of supervision, and a shortage of learning resources, not to mention the traumatic effects of growing up in neighborhoods racked by drugs, violence, crime, and homicide. Hodgkinson reports that a 1990 study by the Census Bureau showed that, of all developed countries, America's children were the most vulnerable in terms of children affected by divorce, youth homicide rate, infant mortality rate, numbers living in poverty, and teenage pregnancy rate. The 1991 final report of the National Commission of Children, *Beyond Rhetoric: A New American Agenda for Children and Families,* states that "poor and minority students from single-parent families and students with limited proficiency in English are at much greater risk in experiencing educational problems and early failure in school, and they are far more likely to drop out of school. These educationally disadvantaged children now account for as many as one-quarter of all American students—and the proportion is likely to grow as the population of low-income and minority children, many of whom live only with their mothers in poor, troubled inner-city neighborhoods, rises over the coming decade."[28]

Both these children and their parents need special services to help with their special problems: strong day-care and health programs, affordable housing and transportation, counseling, and security against crime. All too frequently the services are not available. The problem is compounded by the growing gap between upper-income Americans and the poor or near poor. We concentrate our educational resources on children from relatively stable families, those who are least likely to fail. Discrepancies in per-pupil school expenditures within the United States are greater than in any of our economic competitors. In many states, the amount spent on children in wealthy districts is three or four times that spent on children in poor districts. In New York, the range of public school expenditures per pupil is $3,937 to $10,349; in Texas, $1,848 to $5,243.[29] Supreme Courts in various states are only recently beginning to challenge the inequities.

Moreover, Hodgkinson points out that the charge by the Reagan and Bush administrations that Americans overspend on education is a deception. Americans spend more than other industrialized nations only when *higher* education is included. Huge amounts are spent on higher education, where we have 25 percent of the world's students. If we look only at K–12 expenditures, many nations are investing more in their schooling than we are.[30] Meanwhile, for the bottom one-third of American children in inner-city schools, class sizes are the largest (although the need for individual attention is greatest); physical conditions are often crowded, crumbling, and unpleasant; library, laboratory, and computer facilities are inadequate; physical violence in the neighborhood may intrude into school life; and predictably it is difficult to recruit and retain high-quality teachers and administrators.

After surveying facts like these, and many more, Hodgkinson concludes that the bottom one-third of American children is more likely to fail educationally than the bottom third
of any of our economic competitors. We are crippled—mor-
ally and economically. The president's report on educational
goals for the year 2000 failed to address seriously this central
dimension of our educational problem.

This chapter has demonstrated that we are not devoid
of imaginative educational ideas. But the moral and economic
blight enervating a third of our children cannot be removed
by merely restructuring American schools. The fundamental
issue is whether economic capitalism and political democracy
can muster the will to excise the cancer of poverty that debil-
itates so many of our children. Democratic restructuring of
schools is an important step toward deep reform. It cannot,
by itself, be an answer to the social inequities that drain the
strength of American society.

Nine

The Issues
in Science Education

The basic principle of active methods will have to draw its inspiration from the history of science and may be expressed as follows: to understand is to discover, or reconstruct by rediscovery, and such conditions must be complied with if in the future individuals are to be formed who are capable of production and creativity and not simply repetition.

—Jean Piaget (1973)

As we reflect on what kind of education our children need to prepare them for the year 2000 and beyond, one of the critical questions concerns the kinds of experience they will have in learning science. The great transformer of the modern era is science and the technologies accompanying it. Twenty-first-century people will have to be at home with science and the power of computer technology. The tension between the two waves of educational reform—roughly paralleling the tension between automating versus informating in industry—is much in evidence in debate about science education.

Ken Michaels of the Bureau of Human Resource Development of the Miami-Dade County schools has articulated the deep issue: "The clear message of second-wave reform is that we need to examine our basic philosophical beliefs about teaching, learning, the nature of human beings, and the kinds of environments that maximize growth for teachers and students alike."[1] The "restructuralists," like Michaels, endorse the activist, discovery, or constructivist approach to learning advocated by the Swiss psychologist/educator Jean Piaget.

121

It is obvious that this style is opposite to the school learning described by a British student of organizations, Charles Handy:

> To be a pupil in a large school is a strange experience. How many of us, if asked to organize an office, would so arrange things that people worked for eight or nine bosses in a week, in perhaps five different work groups, in several different rooms, without any desk or chair to call their own or put their belongings and discouraged, if not prohibited, from talking to anyone while working? Furthermore, which of us would then interrupt them thirty minutes into each task and move them on to the next? Only slightly caricatured, that is the experience of a pupil in a large secondary school.
>
> The truth is that, organizationally, the secondary school is not organized around the pupil as *worker* but around the pupil as *product*. Raw material is passed from work station to work station, there to be stamped or worked on by a different specialist, graded at the end, and sorted into different categories for distribution. . . . [Many] leave alienated by an institution that seems to them oppressive, irrelevant, and dismissive of their possible contribution to the world.[2]

Dewey's View of Science

Earlier in this century John Dewey, like Piaget, in searching for a model of effective learning, had turned to the process of "doing science" by the scientific community. He found it to be congruent with values of democratic community. Before turning to contemporary commentary on the state of science education, we may note Dewey's view of what we can learn from science as a learning enterprise. His basic hunch was that the essence of humans doing science authentically is their acting as a dialogical community of inquirers.

In *Problems of Men,* Dewey argued that a more fundamental meaning of science transcends its technical aspects. In its broad sense, it may be seen as a moral ideal and a liberating form of social relationship. Our disillusionment with science is so great that it is hard to listen to such an argument. But to clarify the idea we may note that he made an important distinction between what he called "the scientific temper"—a general style of inquiry and learning—and "scientific technique," his term for science in its functioning in specific disciplines and technological applications.[3]

It was "the scientific temper" that he recommended as a model for effective human learning and ethical guidance for institutional design. It exemplifies our capacity to free our intelligence—to extend our understanding of the world and our condition. It demonstrates, as method, that mind is not an entity but a form of acting in the world. It shows our capacity to get in touch with problematic situations and to create ideas as plans of action that can be tested, tried, and evaluated in dialogue. The "inherent promise" of the movement of science, Dewey said, "looks forward to a time when all individuals may share in the discoveries and thoughts of others, to the liberation and enrichment of their own experience."[4] So Dewey argued for a democratic "industrial intelligence" that would not only help people solve problems at work but help them to understand the scientific principles behind the transformation of work. They have a right to understand.

Beyond that, humans doing science authentically reveal the type of human relations required for creative learning. Dewey argued that the community of science represents an organic union between the needs of freedom and individuality, on the one hand, and community and collective authority on the other. "Science," he said, "has made its way by releasing . . . the elements of invention and of novel creation in individuals . . . who freed themselves from the bonds of tradition." At the same time, the authority of scientific findings depends on its being collectively tested and cooperatively confirmed in the deliberations of free inquiry.[5]

These qualities of the scientific temper—individuality and dialogical community—were the values of a way of living—democratic living—that supported what Dewey called "the dominant vocation" of all human beings: intellectual and moral growth. "Democracy," Dewey pronounced in one of his most famous statements, "is a name for a life of free and enriching communion. . . . [It] is more than a form of government, it is primarily a mode of associated living, of conjoint communicated living."[6] The moral function of institutions is to support that form of living.

In the final analysis, institutions like schools and industries cannot become "good work" places until they support the power of people to learn through "conjoint communicated living" at the site itself. This means we must take seriously the need to create smallness within bigness. In Dewey's words: "The final actuality is accomplished in face-to-face relationships by means of direct give and take. Logic in its fulfillment recurs to the primitive sense of the word: *dialogue*."[7] Thus Dewey, like Gadamer, makes the moral case for a form of postindustrial intelligence that honors us as *homo poeta*, meaning makers, and honors the dialogical inquiry style of learning that supports it.

Science Education Under Scrutiny

In the field of science education, the distinction between a centralized, linearly organized model of learning and the Piaget/Dewey model of discovery and inquiry was sharply sketched in a *New York Times* supplement, "Science Under Scrutiny: When Education Fails" (January 7, 1990). In the critique and recommendations of the scientists and educators, one finds striking parallels to the debates over the design of work in industry.

The depressing picture of the state of science education needs little elaboration: Huge numbers of American students avoid science in both secondary and higher education; 40

percent of high school students who enter college with an intention of pursuing a science career drop out after the first course, 60 percent by graduation; in a recent science test taken by high school students in fourteen countries, American students ranked fourteenth.[8]

Typical of the critics in the *Times* supplement was Bill Aldridge, executive director of the National Science Teachers Association, who noted well-intentioned but counterproductive measures of the 1970s and 1980s. A major effort, he said, was to raise standards by increasing the amount of material to be covered: "What's happening from grade school to graduate school is the suffocation of curiosity under an avalanche of fact." Much of this pressure derives from the epidemic of testing. Teachers feel forced to cover everything that might be on the test. "Testers break science up into small objects. What you get is an unassembling of the most fantastic features of science—its stories, its patterns. You get denudement of everything that's rich and fun and beautiful." The result is millions of children "wasting their time learning virtually nothing of value." The most pressing student question is not about science but "Will it be on the test?" The approach assumes that *covering* science by the teacher adds up to *learning* science by the students. The pressures support a kind of rapid assembly-line coverage of material. It leaves little room for personal engagement, for Socratic dialogue, or for collaborative inquiry and communication. Students who are left in the pipeline are "students who are rewarded for being quiet, for doing what the teacher says."[9]

This view was confirmed by an article reviewing the nature of science textbooks.[10] A writer of science texts reported the pressure put on him to reduce science to terminology employed in tests. He cited an estimate that students are force-fed between 2,400 and 3,000 new terms and symbols per course—a new term roughly every two minutes. It produces dull texts that students hate to read. The result is that science gets reduced to a list of accepted "facts" and "truths." The heart of science is neglected: science as a way of knowing, a way of thinking, a process of observing and refining our understanding of the world—and rejecting ideas that do not hold up under evidence. Seen in this way science, as Dewey said, is a defined model of human learning—an exemplar of humans acting as *homo poeta.* When science study is approached in the spirit of science itself, children can experience themselves as *homo poeta:* as explorers of the wonder of existence. We cheat them of that experience if we reduce the study of science to the banalities of Trivial Pursuit. Teachers accustomed to rapid-fire coverage may find it difficult to change. The *Times* supplement notes that for some teachers the notion of engaging students in intellectual struggle—give and take instead of coverage—may be frightening. "If I do that, I'll lose control" is an often-heard comment (not unlike the comments by beleaguered managers in industry).

If the problem is seen as atomization of instruction and noninvolved students, what are the alternatives? The National Academy of Sciences and the National Science Teachers Association are exploring ideas for designing science studies for elementary schoolchildren. The common goal is to develop the ability to think scientifically, to develop hypotheses, to test and draw conclusions. They agree that the one sure way to teach this is a hands-on approach. They turn to nonschool alternatives for approaches that seem promising. A physicist from Princeton's Institute for Advanced Study recommends as an example the San Francisco Exploratorium, which teaches science concepts by using equipment that can be found around the house. According to the Exploratorium's founder, Frank Oppenheimer, "No one flunks a science museum. Nothing may be more important than an environment in which it is safe to be wrong."[11]

At the secondary level, the American Association for the Advancement of Science has launched a major effort: Project 2061 (*Science for All Americans,* 1989). Teams of teachers and administrators are devising a K-12 science curriculum with the help of computers. The trend is to require study of science, technology, and math in grades K-12, getting students to work in groups instead of as competitors, and getting students to use technology—from hammers and saws to computers. The style of instruction is heavily hands-on with 60 percent of time devoted to lab work and the remainder to discussion. "To get students to make their own discoveries and not read about them in a book—that's what science is all about," said one of the commentators.[12]

Dr. George Campbell of the National Action Council for Minorities in Engineering found that this type of action-oriented learning helps to close the gap between white males, on the one hand, and minorities and women on the other. A model science program involves students in group projects and study sessions where minority students learn to interact with their white counterparts. Campbell says: "One of the major reasons that minority students do not succeed in technical fields is that they fail to become involved in group study activities with their peers. . . . When it comes to science and engineering, which are collaborative efforts, that is critical."[13]

In reaching for alternative ideas, the authors of "Science Under Scrutiny" all point to the need to challenge the *structure* of schools in a way the top-down "reform efforts" of the 1980s failed to do. One of the recommended alternatives was the program of the computer-enhanced Cougar Valley Elementary School of Silverdale, Washington.[14] By combining cooperative team approaches with state-of-the-art technology, the program provides one way of challenging the egg-crate structure and transforming the culture of the school.

Ideas for change came from a brainstorming committee that developed Strategy 2020 involving 150 teachers, administrators, and parents. The goal was to design new ideas and strategies for promoting learning:

- Technology should be available to manage learning and to diagnose, present, and evaluate it. (A grant of $300,000 provided 221 computers for 518 students.)
- Administrative and educational decisions should be made at the lowest level, preferably by teachers and students.
- Teachers should be managers of instruction, not presenters of information.

- Teachers should function as teams of professionals, sharing ideas and communicating frequently.
- Students should become more actively involved in their own learning, both individually and in groups.

For drill on language skills, students spend time in the computer laboratory. At the end of the day teachers get a printout for each student. On the basis of this printout, teachers select the next day's work. The result, a teacher said, is "no more correcting worksheets." The computer helps gear work to the individuals' skill level and frees the teacher to offer personalized instruction and counsel students.

Teachers team-teach with multiple age groups in large rooms organized around five or six learning centers. Students work in small groups, sometimes with a special education teacher or community volunteers. Computers help handle the complexity of these open classes in ways that were not available in the 1960s. Teachers thus become leaders of educational teams that include paraprofessionals, teaching aides, computer lab managers, and volunteers. A voice mail system is being introduced so that parents can call after hours and get oral reports on their children's progress. This feature not only eliminates much of the need for testing, since computer feedback shows where each student stands, but the parent gets the teacher's personal views.

The school's culture is being changed as well by use of a "local area network" that links all the computers in the schools. Teachers use it to record attendance, assemble lunch orders, schedule meetings, and exchange ideas for assignments for particular students. Students write compositions on the computer, work together to produce their own newspaper, and have used computers to organize a production of the *Nutcracker*. The superintendent, noting all this activity, says he now sees that "technology is a license to productivity." He adds that a product's quality is directly influenced by the frequency of informed interaction between a caring worker and the product.

From the Silverton, Washington, school we can see that

the use of computer technology offers new flexibility and power to teachers and students. Even when the computer is used most productively, however, we are only beginning to learn how to live with it. The specter of all the failed promises for educational technology haunts us—the wonders that would flow from a TV set in every classroom, for example, or from performance contracts with corporations who guaranteed results. It has been estimated that 85 percent of current computer use in classrooms is for workbook-style drill. Nevertheless, the impact of computer/communications technology in the 1990s is inevitable. The stakes for both American schools and the computer industry are enormous. We turn next to issues of computer use that will have to be confronted in the near future.

Ten

Computers in the Schools: What Do We Do with Them?

I am still a yellow pad and pencil person. But even I can see that an acceleration of communications/computer technology will go into Fast Forward in the 1990s. As I write this, I have open on my desk an article on "The Information Age Office."[1] It tells me that by the end of the 1990s our offices may be like information control rooms. The telephone, fax machine, photocopier, color printer, and computer will be integrated components in an information appliance. According to AT&T scientists, it will take dictation, receive and review electronic mail, and dispatch letters or memos at specified times. The appliance will display pictures of callers on a high-definition television. In communications via the machine we may combine our voice message to these persons together with copies of memos or articles plus our comments. All this is made possible by the information appliance that shuffles 10 billion or 100 billion byte capacity optical laserdiscs, each capable of storing an entire reference shelf of information. Intelligent software is on the way that can gather information like a good research assistant. Our friendly information appliances will be hooked up via networking to other nearby computers and to global information sources.

Fiber-optic communication will make it easy to transmit billions of bits of data from one coast to another in seconds. Senator Albert Gore, cochair of the Congressional Clearinghouse of the Future, observes: "In many fundamental ways, fiber optics will change the way we view our world, just as the Copernican Revolution did."[2]

This is just a sample of the world that our children now in school will be entering. Clearly there is no specialized "job training" that will equip them to cope. We cannot foresee the kind of future they will confront any more than the Wright brothers in 1903 could have imagined the nature of air travel in the 1990s. It seems equally obvious that the best bet will be to provide young Americans with learning environments that prepare them to be flexible, creative learners with self-confidence about handling the unknown challenges of the electronic path ahead.

What should be the nature of educational technology in formal education? This question is a separate topic in itself. Here I want to concentrate on one key issue relevant to the themes of this book. If we see the introduction of computer technology into the schools as raising certain issues comparable to the impact of high tech in industry, the analogous question, once again, is this: Which strategy of use will be adopted—centralized "automating" or participative "informating"?

The choice will be played out in the responses made to the 1990 National Goals of the Governors' Conference. These goals call simultaneously for fundamental restructuring as well as a dramatic upgrading of national academic achievement. There is an unacknowledged tension in this twofold goal. Restructuring might mean placing the main bet for improvement on decentralizing—with emphasis on features like honoring local school autonomy and teachers' initiatives in designing learning. (Let them work out their own system of reporting on progress.) Or it might mean moves toward a national instructional and testing effort to make educators feel the heat of test score comparisons.

If the focus is on the latter strategy, a logic may emerge that pushes reform toward a national computer system to coordinate curriculum and testing procedures. One can even imagine a nationwide mainframe monitoring for national integration and uniformity. Definite moves in that direction were in the minds of the creators of the governors' report in relation to Goal 3: "By the year 2000, American students will leave grades 4, 8, and 12 having demonstrated competency in challenging subject matter including English, science, history, and geography; and every school in America will ensure that all students learn to use their minds well, so that they may be prepared for responsible citizenship, further learning, and productive employment."[3] To measure progress toward these goals, the report's designers anticipated using tests from the federally sponsored National Assessment of Educational Progress (NAEP). The National Assessment Governing Board has proposed setting "competence" levels for the tests at each of the designated grade levels and expanding the reach of the tests so they can be used to rank states, districts, and perhaps even schools. Some enthusiasts have projected the possibility of using these scores as a means of establishing rewards or penalties to schools and districts.

Such thinking reflects one of the rationales flowing from the National Goals report. The assumption is that if standards are set and incentives established, school people will be forced to produce results. It reflects a lack of trust in educators—the feeling that they do not know how to define the task, or do not work hard enough, or maybe are not competent. Clearly specified goals, the right mixture of sticks and carrots, and national mainframe monitoring might build the necessary fire under them.

That is the path to a more sophisticated return to the early 1980s reform, the failure of which led to the call for decentralized restructuring. By blandly calling for both, the report conveniently ignores the likelihood that the first emphasis may overwhelm the second. The lure of creating a national test score contest may be irresistible. (Japan-watchers should note, however, that the Japanese, who have accomplished much with the Exam Hell strategy, are now conjecturing that it is self-defeating because it fails to engender the inventiveness, flexibility, and creativity required by the new world in the making.) There is no doubt that the computer technology now exists to turn us toward an automating strategy of centralized control. The question is whether the power of computers can be used to facilitate decentralized creative initiatives that produce the *quality* of teaching and learning demanded for our time.

In contrast to the centralized command approach, there is another use that can be made of computer technology. In this chapter, I want to look at one alternative that moves in an *informating* direction—one that combines the democratic with the technical—analogous to democratic sociotechnical theory in work redesign. This alternative is illustrated in the Apple Classrooms of Tomorrow (ACOT) program developed through the Advanced Technology Group at Apple, Inc. It demonstrates that there is a striking potential for transforming classroom learning, but with major cautions. First, it cannot promise a quick fix on a mass scale—the reach for quick results, in fact, will kill it. Second, it requires a full complement of equipment as well as institutional and community support—probably more dollar support than Americans with a weakened economy are prepared to provide. Third, it requires commitment to a set of values—to a nexus of ideas about human learning that is at odds with our mainstream tradition. Even so, it is not an esoteric creation but fits in many ways the style of the Silverton, Washington, schools. Finally, it cannot promise to be "the one right way"—but it does show there is a way to incorporate the power of technology to support interactive, collaborative, inquiring ways of learning, ways that fit decentralized informating rather than centralized automating design.

Because it exemplifies the kind of education that fits many of our critical needs, the ACOT program deserves to be examined at some length. (I take this position even at the risk of being seen as a public relations agent for Apple, Inc.) I have visited ACOT schools in Columbus, Ohio, and Cupertino,

California, and have talked with teachers and students at both sites. While ACOT is not the only way to go, it does illustrate the central importance of guiding the use of computers by a philosophy of learning that can avoid turning computer-assisted instruction into just another technological fix.

What Is ACOT?

Apple Classrooms of Tomorrow, begun in 1985, describes itself as a flexible consortium of researchers, educators, students, and parents working collaboratively to explore, develop, and demonstrate powerful uses of technology in teaching.[4] One aim was to provide volunteer schools with the sort of computer-enriched environment that might be widely available by the year 2000—and to do this in five different types of communities: an elementary school in a wealthy high-tech suburban California community; an inner-city black school in the upper South; an elementary school in rural Minnesota; another in a mixed social class Tennessee community; and an urban secondary school in Ohio. Apple provided selected classrooms with appropriate hardware—for example, a computer at school and at home for each teacher and student; printers, scanners, laserdiscs, and the like; hundreds of software titles; and computer consultants.

A basic question was faced at the outset: How would the project directors and personnel relate to the teachers? The ACOT designers were well aware that while most American schools have some computers, the great majority use them in the same way as workbooks—for drill and remedial work. ACOT could have entered the schools as the expert authority to show teachers a "more correct, creative" usage. The decision was to give active support to teachers who wanted to innovate in their own chosen directions. This meant listening to teachers and talking with them about ideas.

David Dwyer, director of research, and his colleagues were experienced public school teachers. From personal experience they were skeptical about the viability of expert-prescribed reforms. They had respect for the hard-won but often belittled skills of teachers. They respected the courage and integrity it takes to face the sometimes exciting but always exhausting six-hour daily reality—the reality of thirty kids squirming with energy, curiosity, anxiety, and frustration.

Reformers yearn to impose their dreams on teachers. As the "doers," teachers face not only their squirming charges but state-mandated prescriptions, parental expectations, and test score accountability. In the words of the project: "They must survive the day; they must be ready for the next." So they must above all be pragmatists—using what has proved viable for maintaining their authority and getting the job done. The time-honored practices of "real school" furnish the workable tools: lecture, text and workbook seatwork, recitation, testing. The belief that, "all theory aside," this is what schools are and ought to be is anchored in years of participating in schools that we all have experienced. In the words of Theodore Sizer, "They have become so familiar that any other form of providing for the schooling of young Americans seems unimaginable."[5]

Rather than denigrate this reality, the ACOT strategy was to accept it and then support the teachers in the directions they chose to go. At the same time, the ACOT staff, on the basis of their own years of teaching and experience with computers, leaned toward what they called a constructivist view of learning. Central to the discussion of constructivism is the issue of control—the who and how of control. Underlying these control questions are disagreements about the very nature of knowledge and learning. As the ACOT report put it: "From one perspective knowledge is an accumulation of facts and principles that can be communicated to the learner. From another viewpoint, knowledge is personal and must be constructed or discovered by the learner. The first supports the notion that instruction can be an orderly science. The second leads to more idiosyncratic views of teaching."[6]

Five Stages of Evolution

After three years of observation and lively interaction during which the ACOT staff fed in ideas about computer use and information about learning theories and curriculum, each of the five schools had developed its own way of incorporating computer technology into its regular instructional technology such as workbooks, crayons, whiteboards, overhead projectors, TV, and the like. But they also had moved in general toward the constructivist point of view. It is a fair question to ask how much was due to ACOT's influence. Certainly no ideas were imposed. Rather, it appears that the constructivist perspective grew naturally out of teacher/staff reflections on experience with the computer-rich environment. To illustrate the point, let us follow the evolution through the stages of entry, adoption, adaptation, appropriation, and invention.

Entry

At the entry stage, a conventional text-based instructional technology was in place with workbooks, ditto sheets, overhead projectors, and the rest—the support system for the regular routine of "real school" reality. Into this setting came confusion from introducing a new technology (computers, formatting disks, tangled cables, and extension cords) and the disruptions of changing students from familiar routines to learning how to live, physically and socially, with the computers—for example, "children 'mousing around' with the computer when they should be listening." In facing new discipline problems, resource management issues, and personal frustration, one teacher's sour reaction was understandable: "If I had my druthers, I don't think I would ever look at a computer again."

Adoption

Somewhere in the course of the first year, struggles in adjusting to the presence of the new technology gradually shifted to acceptance. Teachers and students mastered the many skills and ideas of successful computer use, and then put them into play to support text-based drill-and-practice instruction. The familiar pattern of lectures, individualized seatwork, and recitation continued as before—and understandably so. Teachers faced with state mandates and standardized testing can be expected, for survival reasons, to go with what they know gets the job done. They were surprised, however, to learn that, despite the confusion, traditional test scores showed no decline. Teachers were encouraged to find that attendance was up, discipline problems were down, and measures of self-esteem and motivation were strong—a warranty for continuing.

Adaptation

This stage was marked by greater productivity in the use of computers. A fourth-grade teacher reported that many students could now type faster than they could write. There was an outpouring in the amount of writing, and students willingly reworked their papers. A high school chemistry teacher reported that his students were learning to write and balance chemical formulas faster and more accurately than before. On many assignments, students no longer used pencil and paper. One teacher reported:

> They download [the teacher's] handouts to the computer, work on tasks assigned, and send the final copy of their work to the printer to be picked up by [the teacher]. No more pages and pages of handouts that are lost, replaced, and lost again.

In fact, many students were getting hooked on computers, as evidenced by comments like:

> We are finding that students are coming in to use the computers during lunch and staying late to complete their HyperCard assignments on the countries they are researching. This degree of commitment and engagement is really unusual in a group of quite ordinary kids.[7]

Appropriation

In the second year, teachers and students were moving toward appropriation—to the point where they were coming to understand and use technology comfortably to get real work done. (As the root word *proprius* (self) indicates, "to appropriate" is to make it one's own.) A couple of examples may illustrate the point. One second-year teacher:

> I could not believe how labor saving it was, and now I believe, like many other teachers who have discovered the same thing, that it would be hard to live without a computer. If you had to take away the computer I have at home, I would have to go out and buy one. . . . It has become my way of life.

As teachers became thoroughly familiar with the computer themselves, they got excited about new ways of getting their students involved:

> It runs like a charm. . . . Now we can simulate a newspaper company. Eventually students will work in groups, each with its own task, some for art, business graphics, articles, and the editing group. Students can place finished work in a public share desk for the editing group to retrieve and complete the publication.[8]

The trend was toward engaging students in more collaborative, creative ways that combined interdisciplinary projects, individualized instruction, and team teaching. A study of a city culminated in a scale model of a downtown business district with four-foot-tall buildings and robotic elements run by twelve Macintosh computers. Eventually, this project led to field trips to specific buildings and research about businesses and the people who work there.

As projects like these emerged, teachers came to see

their students' highly involved skill with technology, their ability to learn on their own, and their gradual shift from competitive to collaborative work patterns. When it worked, teachers made comments like:

> It's amazing to me how much these kids are learning. . . . Kids are doing things that are not assigned. The excitement is that they are motivated, seeing the power of the things which they are learning how to use, creating for themselves solutions to problems for other things. That is the goal of the educator. That the student be motivated to solve problems important to him, not to go after points. You never see this in regular classes.[9]

As both teachers and students came to appropriate the technology, respect for each other's expertise evolved and roles began to change. Student and teacher roles could shift in the process of getting work done. An observer noted:

> The teacher began to explain a method he used which was pretty involved, when about eight students began saying, "No, no, no. All you have to do is . . ." The teacher was delighted that now he has supporters who can help him as they discover shortcuts with the software.
>
> The interactions of children at computers were different. Specifically, students talked to each other more, they frequently asked for assistance from their neighbors, they were quick to interrupt their own work to help someone else, and they displayed tremendous curiosity about what others were doing.[10]

Invention

With the stages of entry, adoption, adaptation, and appropriation as part of their experience, by 1990 the groundwork had been laid for invention. ACOT observers noted an increasing tendency of teachers to reflect on teaching, to question old patterns, and to speculate about the reasons for changes occurring in the students. All this provided the conditions for undertaking even more effort. Looking back from the vantage of 1990, a staff member summed up what was going on:

> Though variation exists, the staff of ACOT's classrooms are more disposed to view learning as active, creative, and socially interactive processes than they were when they entered the program. Knowledge tends to be held more as something children must construct and less like something that can be transferred intact. The nature of these teachers' classrooms, the permissions they have granted their students, and their own instructional behaviors demonstrate that shift in action.[11]

This statement indicates the potential for institutional change made possible by the ACOT way of introducing a new technology: through involvement. But it glosses over the anxiety and struggles of the people actually asked to do the pioneering.

It is worth noting that we are talking here about a subset of the larger social change at issue in this book: the effect on the quality of life caused by the introduction of electronic technology. In education, it is a matter of introducing a new technology into an established rule-controlled "real school" tradition. In the ACOT project, an effort was made not to reform by an external imposing of technology on pliant clients. It was more in the style of democratic sociotechnical work theory. The assumption, then, is that human systems are "socio" as well as "technical." Not to take full advantage of the distinctively human potential for collaborative, creative involvement is to cheat ourselves of exploring the full power of the system for improving practice—and the quality of life in the system.

The next point is to recognize the *difficulty* of the task of changing from the beliefs and practices of one system to the other. ACOT accepts that school change does not occur just by rational command. Instructional evolution is not a matter of abandoning beliefs but of gradually replacing them with more relevant beliefs shaped by experiences in an altered context:

> Instructional change can only proceed with a change in beliefs about instruction and learning. Teachers' beliefs can only be modified while they are in the thick of change, taking risks and facing uncertainty. Teachers bold enough to participate in these efforts require and deserve modifications in their organizations' structure: alterations that permit and encourage peer observation, dialogue, and reflection. Most importantly, they must have a way to gain continued assurance that their struggles are worthwhile.[12]

ACOT in Action: Two Case Studies

ACOT researchers did two case studies illustrating what can happen under different conditions. Both demonstrate that the path of change is not neatly linear but a series of periodic ventures into new terrain—sometimes with the satisfaction of success, sometimes with frustration or failure leading to retreats before new advances.

Mrs. Smith was a fifth-grade teacher in an inner-city school with a strong traditional orientation. Hers was a first-year effort in a self-contained classroom with little opportunity to discuss with others what she was trying to do. In fact, she sensed that her colleagues, administrators, and even her family were critical of her efforts. But with a great deal of courage she passed through the stages and had gained a sense of appropriation before the year was over. It was a rocky road. At the entry and adoption stages, she used the computers to complement her routine. She presented a lesson and then allowed the children to use the computer for individualized practice and reinforcement drills.

Midway in the fall term, she began small-group instruction and suggested a class newspaper that would allow students to choose editors and reporters and, in large part, run the project. She felt good about children taking responsibility and developing their skills with computers. By December she could note in her journal:

> I do not have the discipline problems that I have had in the past or that my friends are having this year, and I think the factor that I would say made the difference is the computer. Students are getting immediate feedback; they're busy; the work is more appropriate because they have varied activities. I have more time to deal with problems.

She continued to alternate her regular routine with computer involvement, feeling good about a satisfying science activity where children were working together under their own direction. But she developed qualms about some new things that threatened her regular expectations:

> Lots of noise results from the interaction of computer activities: children talk, move around more than in conventional classrooms. Keeping noise and movement controlled is necessary. . . . The availability of software at individual work stations gives students too much control over what they elect to do. Some students choose to do things that are not relevant at the time.[13]

The youngsters settled down when she returned to lecture and recitation activities and reverted to her assertive discipline program with its tokens for good behavior. By midyear she began to open up her class once more—with opportunities to work together with a broader choice of tools. The class newspaper was going well again—but with noise despite control efforts:

> The newspaper articles show progress. I proofed the articles and found only one comma missing. The kids are working well together. . . . But the noise level interfered with a reading group.

Another day she reported:

> Everybody was working merrily away. Brenda was sucking her thumb with one hand and typing with the other. That was quite funny. I asked a friend to video this because it had never happened before. The kids were just typing away. All you could hear was the sound of the typing keys. It was just wonderful.

But she continued to be bothered by the "commotion":

> Using the printers requires students to break out of regimented behavior patterns. They are not used to such freedoms, which creates lots of commotion.[14]

Mrs. Smith continued to struggle with an inner conflict as the year progressed—a conflict between her former belief in how a classroom should function and her new perception of other possibilities made possible by a classroom radically altered by computers and boxes of software. Although she enjoyed seeing students motivated by the new materials, she grew uneasy as they challenged the old assumptions—not through insurrection but by their clamor to work at things that were fun and useful. It is unsettling to find that the old ways no longer apply. ACOT researchers summed up Mrs. Smith's first-year experience:

> A cycle was created in which she initiated an innovation that led to both intended and unin-

tended outcomes. These outcomes made her world more uncertain, raising her personal anxiety which led to questions about the basic premise on which she based her attempts to innovate. She reduced the dissonance by returning to behaviors that were consonant with her beliefs but then encountered resistance from her students, who preferred the more innovative activities to the traditional ones. Moving to reduce this source of dissonance, she would, again, attempt a more innovative path until her anxiety level rose once more. The process was exhausting.[15]

Mrs. Smith retired from the ACOT project at the end of the first year.

The second case study involved Mrs. Brown, a teacher in another ACOT school. She followed a similar path with switchbacks between her conservative beliefs about teaching and the new possibilities she found in the peculiar new computer-filled classroom. The process was exhausting for Mrs. Brown, too, but she did not leave the project. Indeed, she seemed to gain confidence about her new pedagogical style as she continued year after year with ACOT.

Mrs. Brown, however, had a significantly different context in which to begin her ACOT work. She came to the program in its second year, after the first-year teachers had developed firm convictions about joint planning, interdisciplinary instruction, and team teaching. This advantage gave Mrs. Brown constant opportunities to watch other teachers in action and to talk with them informally. Moreover, she received reassurance and strong encouragement from her principal and the district technology coordinator. With this kind of support and backing, Mrs. Brown could experiment and grow in spite of periodic setbacks. Whereas Mrs. Smith became a pioneer without support from the school, family, or neighborhood, Mrs. Brown had the backing of a school culture that gave her continual support for handling the fears that go with change.

We can see that teachers in the process of change are affected by the attitudes of co-workers and the belief systems of the school and community. If there is no change in the system itself, the teacher, struggling to innovate, may be overwhelmed by frustration and feelings of abandonment. The ACOT project reveals some minimal conditions for survival. First, teachers in the entry stage need technical training about the technology itself. Second, as they get more deeply involved they need opportunities to reflect on the consequences of their efforts. They need the opportunity to talk with fellow professionals about their ideas on learning and instruction and exploring more powerful learning experiences for their students.

We can see, too, that the students themselves were going through parallel experiences. Confronted with the new computer environment, they were drawn into forms of learning in which they took risks and opened themselves to surprises. To do this, they needed the chance to interact collaboratively, to engage in dialogue, to reflect on the meaning of what was happening, and to project new ideas to explore. They became interested in listening to each other. They were willing to help each other, and to be helped, in order to get the work done. Being drawn to the work for its own sake was quite different from working individually and competitively for "extra points." We do not have to look far to see the connection between the style of learning of these students and the way a computer programmer described his view of his work:

> Anyone who works as a computer programmer and wants to advance is always learning in everything he does. Because the way you become a valuable programmer is through the extent of your knowledge base of different types of systems and different techniques in programming. . . . That's pretty much seen as part of all programming work: either you are learning from someone or you are teaching someone else because they want to learn from you.[16]

The Computer Chronicles Network

That the ACOT experience is not unique is confirmed by a study of the effects of computer usage on classroom dynamics by H. Mehan in 1989. It was a study of four elementary school teachers whose classrooms were equipped with computers. In his yearlong observations, Mehan found that, as in ACOT, the teachers began by incorporating the computers into their regular classroom teaching styles. But noteworthy things began to happen when the teachers tied in their computers to a student news wire service known as the Computer Chronicles. This electronic news network, connecting students from Alaska, California, Hawaii, Israel, and Mexico, is modeled on the international news wire services. Students at each site write, edit, and store articles on floppy disks that are sent to all participating sites. Students at each site combine their own articles with ones written elsewhere to produce their own local newspaper.

The Computer Chronicles network thus gives teachers a chance to create learning environments that are functional—where reading and writing goes on to get work done, not just to get a teacher's grade. Teachers found that students took more control over their writing when they realized their work would be read by a widely scattered audience of their peers. Moreover, students became active in editing and revising their own stories and those of their classmates. The articles selected by an editorial board, composed of five to eight students, were sent over the news wire to students elsewhere. Here another review process occurred to decide if articles submitted would appear in the local newspapers.

It is not surprising that the students became highly motivated and a new social structure was created giving them more control over what and how they learned. Mehan summarizes the new participation structure that emerged in the classrooms:

> Teachers placed two students together at the computer. Peer interaction emerged from this arrange-

ment. Students worked together without direct supervision. They were left to their own devices to sort out the manner in which tasks would be completed. While students were responsible for completing their assigned work at computers, the students worked out the details of task completion themselves, resulting in voluntary instead of compulsory forms of instruction activity. Since the teachers did not monitor the students' work at the computer directly, their work was evaluated privately instead of publicly. As a consequence of this change in participation structures, students developed a different sense of social relations. They assisted each other at the computer and cooperated to complete assigned tasks.[17]

As the new collaborative work style of students, both at ACOT and in the Computer Chronicles network, replaced teacher-directed instruction, it might be taken as a threat to the teacher's authority. It might also, however, be seen as a way of gaining a new form of authority by giving away an old one. Both in classrooms like these and in high-tech industry, the threat to hierarchical authority can become intolerable for some people. Retreat to a centrally controlled system is possible, of course, but at a cost—at the cost of surrendering the potential for better work and a more fulfilling quality of life.

The Deeper Meaning of ACOT

A program like the ACOT project has obvious interest for the school restructuring effort. It seems fitting to end this chapter with a statement by the manager of the ACOT project, David C. Dwyer. Here Dwyer sets forth the lessons he thinks ACOT researchers have learned as well as warnings that should be noted by national policymakers:

> The purpose of ACOT is to conduct longitudinal research about education and technology that

goes far beyond the simplistic notions of computers as teaching machines. For the past five years ACOT has been working to discover and demonstrate powerful ways to use a variety of technologies to help teachers teach and kids learn. Our partners include more than 45 teachers, 1,000 students, a half a dozen school districts, and researchers from two dozen universities and R&D agencies.

ACOT recently had the pleasure of hosting Governor Booth Gardner and the steering committee of the Education Commission of the States at the Dodson Elementary School in Nashville, Tennessee. The future that Governor Gardner saw included third- and fourth-grade students and special-education students learning energetically and successfully with a variety of technologies.

In the process of developing a futuristic learning environment at the Dodson School, as well as at our other sites, ACOT has learned a great deal about teaching and learning, about the evolution of instruction in immediate-access-to-technology classrooms, about teacher development, and about the critical role assessment plays in any effort to bring fundamental change to America's classrooms.

Our lessons include:

- The use of technology does not guarantee fundamental change in the teaching–learning process and consequently in learning outcomes. It can make the traditional classroom more efficient, more fun, and can raise test scores—when it is used purposefully to that end.
- Technology becomes a powerful tool for fundamental change in education when teachers

shift their roles to learning facilitators, and when they engage children in knowledge-building tasks.

- Supporting teachers in that shift is a major task involving not only training and reeducation, but altering teachers' personal beliefs about schooling. It is a far more difficult task than integrating technology into the classroom.

- Teachers who make the commitment and change their approach to a more integrated and problem-solving one are severely hampered by traditional forms of assessment that emphasize basic skills and memorization of isolated facts. When their students demonstrate new learning outcomes such as creative problem-solving strategies or expertness, teachers find that traditional tests fail to measure these types of student gains and show no significant difference after all their effort. Saddest of all, teachers may be so frustrated by the inflexibility of the assessment system that they return to a direct instructional approach that does affect test scores.

What's wrong with this picture?

In recent years we have recognized that our assessment system is not the tool we wish it to be. As a measure of individual success and progress, it seems more sensitive to student background than student effort in the classroom; as an indicator of future student success, it is notoriously unreliable; as a measure of the efficacy of instructional systems, it is insensitive to different instructional approaches and classroom climates; and it consumes inordinate amounts of instructional time.

Standardized tests—because they don't reli-

ably measure higher-order cognitive skills—
emphasize the acquisition of basic skills and dis-
jointed facts. If basic skills are the standard by
which teachers and their students are to be
judged, teachers sensibly emphasize basic-skill
instruction. The worse their students perform on
these tests, the more they emphasize basic skills,
and the more they lament that they don't have
time to work with their children in more meaningful and interesting ways.

Thus already disadvantaged students, who
perennially perform the poorest on standardized
tests, receive more and more instruction that car-
ries them further and further away from any
chance of becoming the thinking citizens, problem solvers, and information managers that
society requires in the next century. Because these
very children represent one-third of the work
force for the year 2000, this issue is of critical
importance.

More of the same begets more of the same

Goal 3 Resource Group's central message
is loud and clear: Set standards, test achievement
against those standards, and reward on the basis
of improved test scores. History demonstrates that
this message only discourages teachers from working with children in ways that develop higher-
order cognitive skills. By creating national cur-
riculum-based standards in five discrete content
areas and a high-stakes context that encourages
the ranking of schools, communities, states, and
even countries—despite known methodological
problems that make such comparisons invalid—
the Goals Panel risks averting the nation's attention and energies to superficial reforms when our
educational system is in need of deep structural
change.

ACOT's message from the future is that when teachers become facilitators of learning, when instructional tasks become multidisciplinary and open-ended opportunities to pursue solutions to complex and challenging problems, when students are encouraged to work collaboratively and to reach out beyond their classrooms for information and perspective, and when students and teachers have access to communication and information-processing tools—in short, when classrooms are transformed—kids change for the better. Their attitudes toward school changes for the better. What they choose to do and the way they accomplish their work changes for the better. What they believe about themselves and their potential changes for the better. ACOT has also demonstrated that existing measures do not capture these advances.

Painfully, we have watched those changes extinguished in some of our schools where testing and curriculum demands prevented teachers from taking risks. Conversely, in ACOT programs where assessment was treated as a developmental and emergent part of an innovation strategy, teachers became more reflective about their teaching, more attentive to changes in their students, and more strategic about classroom change. Changing the form of assessment can change instruction and student outcomes.

Two points seem critical to the attainment of Goal 3. First, assessment must be considered in broader terms. Achievement tests are important indices of student progress, but they are one-dimensional. ACOT students generally show growth in eight equally important areas: computer use; effective communication; social awareness and confidence; independence; experimentation and problem-solving abilities; dynamic exploration and representation of information; expertness; and positive orientation to the future. Capturing these attributes of student progress requires multiple forms of assessment: portfolios, expositions, demonstrations, and performances. Somehow we must include all of these in our accounting of student and school progress. This is a demanding agenda.

Second, policymakers need to be better informed about the limitations of test scores as bases for important decisions about education. This panel should demand from the assessment profession more comprehensive means for viewing individual growth and systemwide progress of educational improvement.

Changing the form of assessment can break a vicious and destructive cycle that has driven our schools to the lowest common denominator of instruction during the past twenty years. We simply can't afford to continue along the same path.[18]

Facing the Fundamental Choice

By the year 2000, being at home with computer technology will be a prerequisite not only for opportunities in the workplace but for full participation as a citizen. This chapter has shown that schools and educators face a fundamental choice in the way they will introduce our young to computer technology. It can be used as a technical tool to secure learning in relatively mechanical ways; as such it can be geared to channel energies to raise test scores. Or it can be used creatively as part of a more participative, constructivist, sociotechnical style of work and learning. We need the latter approach— both for the flexibility it can bring to America's workplaces and for the quality of fulfillment it can bring to the people using it. To help students become effective with it requires commitment to the idea of people as constructors of ideas.

The temptation to accept the more mechanical approach will be strong. It promises a shortcut to the simple goal of "getting numbers up," and it satisfies the control needs of central administration. In the next chapter, we shall see that a similar choice confronts us in the decisions we make about the design of vocational education for "the world's work."

Eleven

Vocational Education: An Instrument for Educational Transformation?

Controversy has always swirled around vocational education. Lauded by the unsophisticated, panned by the professionals, and shunned by the upwardly mobile, occupational education has been the Lawrence Welk of public education—tolerated and occasionally patronized by the Establishment, but never really accepted.

—Kenneth Gray (1991)

Congress has provided some of the resources and tools that are needed to rebuild and reorient vocational education. Indeed the new law could have the effect of drawing vocational education into the larger movement to reform the whole of American education.

—John G. Wirt (1991)

I want to explore the unlikely hypothesis that the Carl D. Perkins Vocational and Applied Technology Education Act Amendments of 1990 contains the potential for a conceptual restructuring of vocational education—and, beyond that, offers fresh hypotheses for the liberalizing of general education. I make such a claim on the basis of examining particulars in the 1990 legislation—especially the kinds of shifts proposed since the drafting of the initial law in 1984. My argument will be that the proposals, first for vocational education and then for public education in general, reflect an accelerating awareness in the late 1980s that we really have crossed over into an electronic/communications era—a post-industrial era that will not permit us, without heavy penalty, to cling to outdated industrial styles of thinking and practice. And it opens possibilities for strengthening democratic values and practice in order to cope with fast-moving technical realities.

Before exploring particulars, though, I want to take a detour through an event that dramatizes the point: the hundred-hour desert war in the Persian Gulf of March 1991. Alvin and Heidi Toffler, reflecting on its meaning, called it a Third Wave war. This Third Wave warfare is a historic successor to the grisly hand-to-hand killing of First Wave war that arose with the nation-states of the agricultural revolution and the Second Wave slaughter of industrial-era warfare culminating in World War II in which 388,000 civilians, on average, lost their lives every month from 1939 to 1945. While human killing is just as brutal in new form as in old, a new type of electronic-directed warmaking did emerge in the desert in 1991. It was a consequence of the Third Wave economy which replaced the mass production that had produced the tanks and bombers that flattened cities and countryside in World War II. The latest warfare represented "the triumph of silicon over steel," in the words of John E. Pike of the Federation of American Scientists. "What's making all this work," said James F. Digby of the RAND Corporation, "is weapons based on information instead on firepower. It greatly reduces the tonnage of explosives you have to send over."[1] Industrial-era-type Iraqi warriors armed and trained by the Soviet Union were numbed and overwhelmed by a combination of old-time heavy-bomber carpet bombing and new-style precision: information/knowledge-driven weaponry. The unreal shortness of the Nintendo war occurred because a third-rate Second Wave army was hopelessly outmatched by a brilliant Third Wave operation. The old Buck Rogers comic strip might be our best clue regarding a future clash between two fully matched Third Wave forces.

That new weaponry, in part, reflects the customized, microchip, intelligence-driven modes of production that have replaced the Willow Run type of assembly line—a kind of production where microchips and information feedback equips everything from automobiles to microwave ovens with memory, programmability, and a modicum of intelligence. Old-time mass production is rapidly being replaced by de-massified, customized production targeted for "niches" in the market—niches that themselves are subject to constant change. Indeed, the Third Wave military force mirrors

changes occurring in the electronic economy just as the
armies of the earlier agricultural and industrial revolutions
mirrored those economies.

The Third Wave warfare that we saw in Iraq required
incredible orchestration to integrate air, sea, and land operations and coordinate precision-targeted weapons with rapid
deployment, mobility, maneuver, and interdiction. The revolutionary transfusion of knowledge into warfare forced
changes in organization, training, tactics, intelligence, tim-
ing, and battlefield management, as well as reconceptualiza-
tion of the roles of firepower, time, space, logistics, and
communications. In Toffler's words: "What has been acted
out on the deserts of Kuwait and Iraq is so precision
planned, so tightly integrated, so dependent on instant communication, that no previous war in history offers appropriate comparison."[2]

Once Iraqi radar and surveillance were knocked out,
that army was reduced to mere machinery against an electronic system with internal feedback, communication, and
self-regulatory adjustment capacities. It was, in fact, a *thinking* system from command headquarters in the field and in
Washington right down to the lowest-ranked soldiers in the
field. As Marine Col. W. C. Gregson, Military Fellow at the
Council on Foreign Relations, put it, the combat arms soldier

> is not a mere ammunition mule and bullet hose
> holder. He understands both mechanized and foot
> soldier tactics. He is skilled in the operation
> capabilities of helicopters and fixed-wing aircraft,
> for he is most often the controlling agent. Direct-
> ing aircraft means he understands anticraft weap-
> ons. He is skilled in geometry and navigation, to
> direct mortars and artillery—armor and antiar-
> mor, mine and countermine weapons and tactics,
> use of demolitions, computers, motor vehicles,
> laser designators, thermal sights, satellite com-
> munications gear, and organization of supply
> and logistics are part of his kit.[3]

It is a new world in both military affairs and industry. In Toffler's words: "Mindless warriors are to Third Wave war what unskilled manual laborers are to the Third Wave economy—a vanishing species." Having said all of that, one does not have to claim a picture-perfect operation. Anyone who has been in the service knows that it was not by accident that the word "snafu" entered our vocabulary.

We may note that the American "electronic war system" was composed disproportionately of American men and women of color. It was composed, that is, of that portion of our population upon which we will be more dependent in the decades ahead, those of whom we often despair as we see them wasted in the poverty and violence of our ghettos and the human warehouses of our prisons. In American civil life, minority workers are disproportionately represented in muscle work and unskilled labor that in the new economy will be replaced by "smart workers who can operate smart machines." In retrospect, we may see that the 1990 Perkins Act was an effort to respond to realities that had previously not been attended to. It was laying some conceptual groundwork. It is not clear, though, whether we have the will to build on it.

Background of the 1990 Perkins Act Amendments

In September 1990, a month after the beginning of Operation Desert Shield, Congress passed the Carl D. Perkins Vocational and Applied Technology Education Act Amendments.[4] That there was urgency behind enactment is evidenced by the fact that it was passed barely nine months from the start of hearings in the House of Representatives. I believe that if we consider a combination of two factors—the work qualities needed by the Third Wave Army and the situation in civilian life affecting work back home—we can gain insight into why the legislators built into the Perkins Act Amendments features that departed from the historic tradition for vocational education.

Why do I think this vocational education act contains innovative ideas that should be considered by educational policymakers for the system in general? First, there is Toffler's hypothesis that armed forces reflect realities of the economic system. The Persian Gulf warriors give us a clue regarding the requirements of a twenty-first-century work force. The American Third Wave Army needed active intelligence at all levels of operation. It needed sophisticated technical and human communication to provide the flexible responses required to meet a rapidly changing reality. To make the complex system function demanded academic knowledge combined with technical skill. The motivation to meet the achieved level of efficiency came from the need to meet the hard reality of high-tech life. The scientists, technologists, and officers directing the operation could not succeed without collaboration from an impressive capacity for learning "down to the lowest level." People rose to the occasion to gain knowledge and skills at levels that might have surprised their old teachers at Metro High.

Let us combine this glimpse of military forces with features of civilian work life the troops would encounter on their return. Certainly the demographics are changing. As we entered the 1990s, fewer people were entering the work force. While about 2 million entered in 1975, barely 700,000 entered in 1989.[5] As a result of a drop in the number of young entrants, the median age of American workers continued to rise—from 30.6 years in 1982 to a projected 36.3 in the year 2000, with the nonwhite population markedly younger. Youth from minority backgrounds and disadvantaged homes will make up a significantly larger proportion of the youth population. Some 47 percent of new entrants to the labor force (1987) have been white males, and that proportion will decline to under 20 percent. By the year 2000, five-sixths of net additions to the work force will be nonwhites, women, and immigrants. Many of these will be coming from inner-city areas where schools and community life have been blighted by the social neglect of the 1980s. For twenty-three of the twenty-five largest school districts, racial minorities are now the majority of the school population and the numbers of non-English-speaking students is growing. The dropout rate is heaviest in these districts, and high school dropout rates have shown only a marginal decline over the past two decades.[6]

If we compare these features of the emerging work force with changes taking place in the nature of work itself, further clarity emerges. In the steady trend toward a computer-driven society, there continues to be a strong shift from manufacturing to high-tech and service industries. The skills of highly paid factory workers continue to become obsolete. By the year 2000, some 75 percent of employees will need to be retrained in new jobs or taught fresh skills for their old ones.[7] On average, workers now change jobs from four to six times in their work lives. There is a striking trend toward a requirement of more education for the fastest-growing kinds of jobs, those in technical, managerial, and professional areas. A projection of new jobs to be created between 1984 and 2000 shows that more than half will require education beyond high school, with about a third to be filled by college graduates. The median years of education required for new jobs for 2000 will be 13.5 compared with 12.8 for 1984.[8] In absolute numbers, most new jobs will be in service occupations such as administrative support, marketing, and sales. By the year 2000, some 88 percent of the work force will hold jobs in the service sector. While the rate of growth will be greatest in higher-skill areas, the largest *number* of jobs will be for cooks, nursing aides, waiters, and janitors; for cashiers in marketing and sales; and for secretaries, clerks, and computer operators in administrative support. Other than the computer operators, most of these categories require only modest skills. But even here there will be increased expectations that these workers can read and understand directions, do arithmetic, and be able to speak and think clearly. The unskilled clearly will be most vulnerable. The jobs that used to be considered middle-skill level will tend to be considered the new low-skill jobs.[9]

Moreover, smaller firms (under twenty employees), representing only one-fifth of employment, are creating two-fifths of all new jobs. They tend to require people with flexible, multiple skills. Small and medium-sized firms cite the lack of skilled workers as the main reason for not adopting new technologies.[10] In short, under the pressure of new technologies, expanded international trade, and new small businesses, there is a growing demand for people with deeper and broader occupational skills. The primary economic problem for many communities is finding enough people with the new skills required for the new jobs.

The emergence of a single competitive world market with cheaper labor (and technology furnished by international corporations) poses major new challenges if the United States is to maintain a high standard of living. Critical to that end will be the necessity for a strong performance in the rapidly growing high-tech industries. In the early 1980s, less than 5 percent of the output of traditional industries was exported while 40 percent of high-tech output went overseas. These high-tech industries are human-capital-intensive. They employ scientists and technicians to design new products. Other employees have direct contact with customers to keep in touch with demands for new products. Above all, high-tech industry relies heavily on educated workers. In 1980, some 20 percent of high-tech employees had sixteen or more years of schooling, compared to 11 percent in traditional industries, and the relative incomes of those with some post-secondary education had leapt to 100 percent by 1986.[11]

Roger J. Vaughn, an economist with the RAND Corporation, says employers are now recognizing that education imparts the cognitive skills demanded by new processes. Educated workers work better in the production teams required by new technologies. They are more flexible in responding to change. They communicate better with suppliers and customers. They have the foundational knowledge and skills that enable them to acquire new learning as situations require it. Investments in education and job skills are responsible for almost two-thirds of the annual growth in per capita income, which is more than double the contribution of plant and equipment.[12]

In the next ten or twenty years, the need for more effective learning is certain. But there is no sure blueprint for how that learning should be accomplished. There are those who argue that because it is impossible to predict the nature of needed job skills, vocational education before college should be dropped. It should be replaced by more rigorous study centered around the academic disciplines in the manner, for example, of Mortimer J. Adler's Paideia proposal. Then there are those like Roger J. Vaughn of RAND who argue: "Vocational education is no longer an alternative to academic skills. It is vital for everyone's career preparation."[13] The 1990 Perkins Act Amendments moves in the latter direction. I want to explore the argument for that proposal—not because I think the primary function of public education is to furnish the job skills industry needs but because, if properly designed, an integrated liberal and occupational studies program might provide both technical skills and liberal insights to enable our young to make a responsible entry into a postindustrial era.

From what has been said about changes in the nature of work and the work force, several conclusions seem warranted. If we are in a major cultural transition from an industrial to a Third Wave electronics-driven economy, then mere tinkering with specific job skills of the moment is inadequate. Such an approach would reinforce an unfortunate American tendency to concentrate primarily on the effects of technology, instead of a deep understanding of how and why it works. To avoid being alienated by the new, the entire population needs not only technical skills but a kind of learning that provides conceptual insight into the basic transformation of human occupations that is going on around the globe. One way is to get people involved in study and direct participation in broad classes of occupations undergoing change. Ideally, we would look for means of involvement that, like the military for a short time, brought the young together in ways that transcended, at least temporarily, our racial and social class divisions.

In sum, we have a reduced number of work-force entrants and a larger proportion coming from the lower end of the economic-educational scale. We are going to have new expectations for the newer categories of workers who must be tapped to help the United States achieve high competitive quality. Women, for example, by virtue of their growing numbers at work, will move into higher levels of management. A host of problems will arise for them and their families that come from their filling new roles in paid work. Then there are the young men from the hardcore ghettos. They performed well in the Gulf. Others conduct complex and dangerous work in the warfare of the streets. These misused talents do terrible community damage, but they are also reminders of blighted resources a sane society would want to make use of. We cannot afford the moral rot in a democratic society that watches its young destroyed by street war and the brutality of prison. Even if we ignore the human and moral issues, we are wounded in ways our international competitors are not. The Japanese are not spending $20,000 per head every year to incarcerate large numbers of their young men. If we turn to the Perkins Act Amendments I believe we can see that it is an intelligent response to the situation described. It offers new perspectives and new priorities.

The Genesis of Vocational Education

To understand how the Perkins Act Amendments departed from entrenched practice, we need a quick look at features of the mainstream vocational education tradition and how it got that way. The basic framework of federally financed vocational education was established by the Smith-Hughes Act in 1917. Periodic modifications have occurred but in general, as a federally financed component of public education, it has stood apart as a trainer of skills needed by the job market.

Smith-Hughes was an understandable response to the realities of the corporate industrialism that was dominating economic life in the opening decades of this century. The industrial factory system, emerging after the Civil War, swept aside an older agricultural, handicraft, small-town America and replaced it with an urban, corporate, industrial nation. The age-old apprenticeship system that used to welcome young boys when they left primary education was in retreat.

The cities were teeming with non-English-speaking immigrants and a flood of youth leaving the farms. As corporate bureaucracies multiplied in size, young women secretaries were needed to process the flow of paper. While much factory work was deskilled by Taylorism, new skills were demanded by complex, changing industrial machinery. A modicum of literacy was needed by all if for no other reason than to read rules and regulations.

As the disorder swirled, one response to the chaos was a new demand for a formal system of vocational education. One of the earliest proponents of vocational education was the relatively new National Association of Manufacturers (NAM). Its members were motivated by the need to increase their share of foreign markets to overcome the woes of the depression of 1893. Their overseas commercial representatives reported a worrisome, powerful new competitor: Imperial Germany. When they investigated the source of German achievement, they found it in the highly differentiated vocational training programs geared precisely to the hierarchical skill needs of German industry. It was a system separate from the general schools and administered by "practical men" from the Ministry of Commerce rather than by "fuzzy-minded educators." Thus it was a dual system: one system of classical gymnasia and universities for the upper classes and ambitious middle classes, a separate system of practical vocational training for the working classes, directed by leaders of industry who knew what was needed.

Determined to meet the challenge of German efficiency, the NAM set up its own Committee on Industrial Education aimed at securing an American version of German vocationalism. A 1911 report by the committee charged that the work of American schools rested on "theories instead of reality." The schools, it said, offered a literary education that satisfied the one student in thirty who was abstract-minded—and neglected the other twenty-nine. The report maintained, moreover, that practical, no-nonsense German vocational training, run by the industrialists, gave Germany a reliable labor force motivated by a positive work ethic.[14] They were impressed by the words of a leading German philosopher of vocational education: "The first aim of education for those leaving the elementary school is training for trade efficiency, and joy and love of work. With these is connected the training of those elementary virtues which efficiency and love of work have in their train—conscientiousness, industry, perseverance, responsibility, self-restraint, and devotion to an active life."[15]

What a difference such attitudes could make in American factories, where, as the chairman said, "our factory children look upon a shop too much as upon a jail. There has developed among a considerable part of the adult factory workers a dislike, almost a hate, of work."[16] Thus the NAM became convinced that American manufacturers could compete successfully in international markets only if the American school system introduced a set of separate vocational schools guided by men of industry.

A vigorous debate ensued. Ranged in opposition to the NAM was a cohort of democratic progressives—people like Owen R. Lovejoy, secretary of the National Child Labor Committee; Ida Tarbell, queen of the muckrakers who argued for inclusion of girls in industrial education; and, since the fight centered in Illinois, a University of Chicago reform group including George Herbert Mead, Frank Leavitt, and John Dewey. Dewey became the leading spokesman. I reported on the complex debate in *Education in the Technological Society: The Vocational-Liberal Studies Controversy in the Early Twentieth Century.* One major point was that the German dualist system reflected the sharp class division of a European system with a feudal past. Such a separation between the learning of an executive class versus the training of a compliant "hand-minded" working class would violate the aspirations of an American citizenry who rejected Old World social class ideas as inappropriate for a country "where any boy [*sic*] had a chance to become president."

Out of the debate emerged a solution not fully satisfactory to either side: the Smith-Hughes Act of 1917, which generally supported the trend toward separatism. Vocational education was the major aspect of precollegiate education that was to be financed by federal money. It was to be administered by state boards of vocational education ultimately responsible to the federal board directing it. In the main, its thrust was toward developing skill courses designed to meet the vocational needs of an emerging industrial society. Politically the idea was expanded to include such areas as agriculture, which was becoming an industry transformed by science and technology, and home economics and commercial education, which responded to new needs for women. Much of this education was administered separately under the umbrella of federal legislation, but the German pattern was not followed literally. Vocational education was not administered by the industrial community, nor was the sharp dualism of vocationalism versus general education adopted. The distinctively American ideas of a comprehensive high school was projected as a means for bringing together youth of all social classes prior to higher education. Within it, a variety of electives for vocational study were included.

The idea of the comprehensive high school as the unifying, non-class-oriented "people's college" was, of course, never accomplished in reality. The trend toward separate vocational schools and programs became prevalent. A lot of dedicated people designed a variety of skill training programs that provided essential services for American industry. The question before the legislators who enacted the 1990 Perkins Act Amendments was whether the tradition of modifying the basic pattern could be continued or whether new initiatives were required. Given the push and pull of contending interests and forces there was some of each, but bold new thinking did appear with potential for new forms of action for both vocational and liberal studies and their connections.

The Meaning of the Perkins Act Amendments

A perceptive observer of vocational education noted: "The Carl D. Perkins Vocational and Applied Technology Act of 1990 is unlikely to grab the attention of regular educators. But it should. The act is an important step in redirecting vocational education and, ultimately, in restructuring our high schools for the twenty-first century."[17] I want to indicate why I think there is truth in that statement.

Traditionally, vocational education has had the task of teaching marketable job skills to those graduating from high school. Thus vocational education advocates have sought to separate it from the rest of the system. In the 1960s and 1970s, for example, there was a strong effort to establish area vocational schools independent from the high schools. The separation was reinforced by the fact that funding came from federal legislation. The original 1984 Perkins Act did not depart significantly from this tradition. But major changes were introduced in the 1990 legislation in recognition of urgent conditions.

The new law recognizes a fact that could no longer be denied by 1990: The health of a competitive postindustrial society depends not only on the skills of the intellectual and technical elites but on the skills and involvement of the work force as a whole—on the ability of all people at work to learn on the job, to acquire technical knowledge, to solve problems, and to benefit from additional education and training. There is general agreement that we have done a good job with the top 20 percent of high school students. We are in increasing trouble, however, as we fail to bring the rest into full participation. The 1990 Perkins Act Amendments proposed four major changes to get on with that task,[18] changes that could be beneficial to the top 20 percent as well.

First was requirement that funds be concentrated in school districts with the highest proportion of children from poor families. The new provision represents a departure from open-ended expansion of vocational education; it replaces that policy with targeted funding for programs in schools where the need for improvement is greatest. This approach includes integration of fragmented remedial services for handicapped students into a unified effort to serve the diverse needs of impoverished communities.

A second change is in line with the trend toward decentralization of the restructuring movement. Congress specified for the first time that initiatives should come from the local districts instead of the states in setting goals and forming programs for implementation. This is a basic departure from the tradition dating back to Smith-Hughes (1917). Federal law required the *states* to specify training needs, program prescriptions, standards, and means for monitoring conformance by local districts. According to the new law, 75 percent of funds under the basic grant must be distributed to local participants, with 10.5 percent earmarked for state-operated programs for single-parent, displaced homemakers and single pregnant women. Whereas previously only the state plan was required, the local recipients will now be expected to develop their own need assessments and plans for using federal funds. A framework is thus created to give initiative to people who know best the needs and characteristics of economically distressed communities.

A third change focuses attention on national policy regarding the enormous system of postsecondary occupational training. It acknowledges this system's importance by establishing it as a separate program in the federal legislation, but it also incorporates new thinking about how to link it with work in the high schools. This shift is in line with the view that as we approach the year 2000, we can no longer think of a high school diploma as a terminal degree.[19] There is emerging a new mission for occupational training. The long-time practice of teaching specific job skills in high school aimed at full-time employment at graduation is becoming less and less tenable. The Perkins Act Amendments support the "tech/prep" concept—technical preparation in the high school that prepares for postsecondary technical education. This adjustment of the mission of secondary vocational education makes sense in terms of the reality emerging: The percentage of non-college-bound graduates who enter the work force is steadily decreasing while the percentage entering two-year technical education increases. The idea that postsecondary education is necessary for many seems relevant for maximizing the potential of students who will be entering a changing work world. While the Perkins Act Amendments support this development, they continue programs that can give at-risk youth training advantages for entering the labor market upon graduating from high school.

A fourth dimension—potentially the most important—is the call for a new integration of academic and vocational studies. This is a logical development in terms of the trends we have been discussing. The curricular structure that characterized vocational education for the past seventy-five years no longer fits. In that tradition, programs are organized around specific occupational titles and the content is determined by a panel of experts from a particular occupation. When job skills were relatively stable, it served a useful purpose of teaching students how to do jobs correctly. It fit the Taylorist factory model in which production is designed by those who think and executed by those who perform under supervision. It is becoming more and more an anachronism.

Awareness that the emerging work world demands a new kind of learning escalated sharply in the 1980s. In the 1984 hearings for the original Perkins bill, for example, it was considered blasphemy to suggest the integration of vocational and academic education. But by the 1989 Senate hearings, "virtually every commentator noted the need to bring together these two parts of our educational system."[20] The Perkins Act Amendments included potent new requirements: Vocational and academic education should be broadly integrated; vocational education should move from narrow, occupationally specified, skill-based training to instruction in "all aspects of an industry"; vocational education should forge strong links with economic development efforts in the community.

There are examples in the vocational education tradition that fit the new mandate to provide students "with experience in and understanding of all aspects of an industry"—and transferable skills for career changes. One obvious example is the way vocational agriculture has been taught: a combination of instruction and experience in all aspects of running a farm. "Voc ag" students learn to use farm instruments and skills of planting and harvesting; they engage in the study of soil chemistry, botany, animal husbandry, and occupational safety and health; they learn the financing and planning of a farm including concepts like cash flow and marketing, as well as the broader issues of agriculture in modern society. This general idea is applicable in other areas. An automobile program, for example, can be broadened beyond repair skills. Students can study the history of the automobile, see it in terms of the transportation system at large, learn the underlying principles of engine design, study the artistic principles of body design, learn how to operate an auto shop, study the effects of fuel economy on the environment, and learn the meaning of an emerging international auto industry.

Training with a single-skill focus is not adequate for the work world of the 1990s. Workers need general thinking, communications, mathematical, scientific, and technical skills that can be tapped and expanded to confront what is new and problematic. They need to see specialized work in the broad context of industries that will be transformed by computer/electronics processes. They need to know the forces responsible for historical change and how industries are affected by the emerging world economy. They need to be sensitive to energy, safety, and the environment. They need the communications and social skills for living with diversity in the work force. They need the capacity for moving to new levels of responsibility.

But advocates of Perkins-style integration of occupational and liberal studies maintain that the same argument applies to young people in general. They argue that programs which help young people gain insight into the specific, technical, social, and occupational revolutions going on around them can provide a more challenging and liberalizing experience than the standard fare—that the dimension of more active involvement in community life might personally engage more of those students' energy, students who, at present, feel so uninvolved in their studies.

This idea receives support from cognitive scientists who argue that for most people effective learning requires a context that matters to them. Most learning, including workplace learning, takes place in ways quite different from schoolroom learning: It takes place in groups, often cooperatively, instead of by individual effort alone; it relies on using both simple and complex instruments, whereas schools emphasize abstract forms of learning disconnected from objects and the "real worlds" of work, family, and community. School learning often does not connect children's learning to events, people, and objects that have meaning for them.[21] There is evidence too that students who took vocational courses with considerable mathematics content, courses like electronics, agricultural science, and drafting, learned as much mathematics as in traditional courses.[22] What we lack is convincing evidence that programs which require conceptual knowledge applied to real-world tasks can motivate students who are now disengaged.

Talk about "integration" has gone on before. Larry Rosenstock visited a good many schools with claims of integration and found that in most cases it consisted of little more than filling students' schedules with both academic and vocational courses. Acknowledging that fact, the Perkins Act Amendments provided funds for establishing Lighthouse Schools. These would be schools in which liberal and vocational educators would collaboratively design genuinely new programs—programs that would involve youth intellectually and practically with the occupational world of electronic/global change; programs that could challenge the intellectually gifted as well as those with average ability; programs that might be an alternative to the divisive tracking system.

It will not be easy. The traditional isolation of teachers and subjects in the regular schools is one obstacle. The difficulty is compounded by the wide gap in mind-sets between vocational and general educators. We cannot expect miraculous widespread change. What we need are specific visions that challenge the imagination and energies of our creative educators—alternatives to the pressures to simply grind harder to bring up scores. To let these pressures discourage us from bolder tries is to be addicted to self-harm.

There is no single answer to the question of how to improve the secondary school experience for American young people. A number of factors suggest that the integrated academic/vocational Lighthouse programs provided for in the Perkins Act Amendments deserve serious support and exploration as one idea for the nineties.

Integration in Action

Do we have the capacity to create the integrated kinds of learning that the Perkins Act Amendments call for? Time, of course, will provide the answers. There are indications, however, that the recognition of need is a spur to action. Ohio and New York have made important beginnings: Ohio with an extensive program of "applied academics"; New York with its attempts to reform the entire vocational secondary-education curriculum by redesigning it into a continuum of occupational education courses organized around a core curriculum. In the South, the Southern Regional Education Board has formed a consortium of states to develop alternative approaches to the integration of academic and vocational education. A heavy emphasis is being placed on integrated content in principles of technology, applied communication, applied mathematics, and the integration of mathematics and science courses that are being developed by the Center for Occupational Research and Development in Waco, Texas.[23]

If the integrated idea is to have broad appeal, we need working examples of themes that engage the interest and energy of students headed for four-year colleges as well as those who plan to work or pursue technical studies. There is, for example, the Integrated Studies Program (ISP) at the Massachusetts Institute of Technology under the leadership of Arthur Steinberg. The centerpiece of this program is the humanities course, which covers technologies in their historical and cultural perspectives. The thirty or forty freshmen who elect this alternative to the standard curriculum are housed in a special ISP setting that includes study space, lounge facilities, and access to personal computers. It was designed as a family-style setting to establish close faculty/student rapport.

Steinberg, a professor of archaeology trained at Harvard, the American School of Classical Studies in Athens, and the American Academy in Rome, says that broadening students through extensive reading and direct experiences is central to ISP's mission: "With modern technology possessing more and more power, it behooves those charged with its development to be socially responsible for their research and production. They cannot grow to be responsible engineers unless they understand the connections between science and humanity."[24] During the first year, these young men and women are taken through six increasingly complex technologies: cooking, weaving, smithing, clocks, internal combustion engines, and computers. In addition to two-hour classes twice per week there are field trips and twice-weekly hands-on workshops on the technologies.

The first technology, cooking, is studied across cultures. Students cook, study foods, food preparation, and preservation—how technology is affecting cooking. There is a heavy amount of reading ranging from the Bible and *The Canterbury Tales* to *Consuming Passions: The Anthropology of Eating* and *The Joy of Cooking*. Students consider what food has meant in various social and religious contexts. They learn the chemistry of bread making. In learning wok cooking, they study heat transfer and oxidation as well as Chinese culture.

Cooking is followed by weaving. Here students are exposed to the hand-weaving culture of the Andes through readings, films, and workshop experiences. And they visit the empty hulks of the giant mills at Lawrence, Massachusetts, where, in the early 1900s, tens of thousands of textile workers labored long hours under horrendous noise conditions to eke out a bare existence.

The third technology is smithing. Study ranges from archaeological study of Iron Age artifacts and farming tools to Japanese samurai swords. And there is the doing of blacksmithing itself.

The first technology of the second semester is clocks and timekeeping. It includes the history of timepieces, the meaning of time in different societies, and concepts of efficiency and cosmological time. Students disassemble and reassemble a Westclox clock (which they learn was made in China). Their reading culminates in Stephen Hawking's *A Brief History of Time: From the Big Bang to Black Holes.*

The fifth technology, the study of various types of combustion engines, culminates in the disassembly and assembly of Briggs & Stratton engines that are then popped onto go-carts for a spring derby.

The final unit—computers—has been redesigned each year of the program's six-year existence because "there are so many ways they interact with society." Excited about the program and convinced that it has relevance for young children, Arthur Steinberg and his colleagues invited seventeen Cambridge teachers from kindergarten through the twelfth grade to participate in a summer workshop in 1990. As they were bilingual teachers, Steinberg challenged them to create integrated curricula based on their own cultures. One of their programs used Haitian musical instruments to explore math concepts and the science of sound; in another, Portuguese cooking was related to a study of foods and nutrition. Some high school teachers formed their own Center for Integrated Studies aimed at helping fellow teachers construct similar learning units.

At the secondary level, the Rindge School of Technical Arts, Cambridge, Massachusetts, illustrates a parallel idea for younger adolescents. Larry Rosenstock, the director, and his colleagues work closely with Arthur Steinberg and faculty at MIT. They are developing an integrated program at the ninth-grade level around the occupation of architecture and city planning: "Creating Cambridge."[25] The Rindge School, which began as a Latin school in the 1600s and became the Rindge School of Technical Arts in 1888, has a rich tradition of respect for education that is technical and liberalizing. Its aims are simple: to get students to combine their hands and their heads in studying mechanical arts, as these relate to academic and fine arts, and to understand technology and its role in economic and social history.

Rosenstock and colleagues were among the first in the country to design an integrated technical arts education that can apply to secondary students in general. Thus the Rindge School could become one of the Lighthouse Schools called for in the 1990 Perkins Act Amendments. The faculty describes the design of "Creating Cambridge" as follows:

> The curriculum is interactive, cooperative, and project based. Throughout the course students will work together in teams to create "artifacts" of Cambridge—for example, photographs, tapes, painted backdrops, scale models of interiors and exteriors. In other words, Cambridge will be the "text" as students share what they know about the city in which they live, and learn to view the city through new lenses. In the process, students will learn many skills, related to other academic and vocational disciplines—from measuring and architectural drawing to interviewing and creating oral histories. [The work will] culminate in a final public production: presentation of the year's work.[26]

The 120 students in the program are divided into sections of 25 or 30 with "work crews" of 4 or 5 students in each section. Four or five faculty are given time daily to plan and coordinate activities and projects. They work with the students more as coaches and colearners as students go out into the community. In the community, students conduct interviews, spend time in settings where related technical skills are practiced, and do research at Cambridge museums and libraries. The year's work is divided into four units.

In Unit I, "Personal and Neighborhood Views," students begin the year by creating a giant wall map of the city on movable masonite panels that identifies neighborhoods and landmarks. Students develop photographs and edit videotapes in which they identify the "bests" and "worsts" of the Cambridge neighborhoods. They create various "Guides to

Cambridge"—for example, "A Skateboarder's Guide," "A Toddler's Guide," and so on.

In Unit II, "Cambridge Close Up," students begin to take a closer look at the life and industries of the city by selecting specific Cambridge street scenes. They make videotapes and write about the character of the street and its history. In the process, they begin to learn the vocabulary of city planning and design, as well as skills in representational drawing, painting, design, and construction. In this unit, they become "undercover" investigators searching out interesting details of street life and learning how to present their results in scale and in written or artistic form.

In Unit III, "Inside Cambridge," students in small groups learn to do floor plans and work on scale models of buildings that relate to trades and industries. They might, for example, learn how to design a hospital emergency room. In this unit, by interviewing workers and managers, they investigate how design of space affects the people who work within it. They extend their vocabulary of planning, architecture, and design and improve their skills in representational drawing, design, and construction.

Unit IV, "Cambridge Now and Later," is a culminating unit. Now students bring together the products of many teams and individuals in models of the landscape of city blocks. The focus is on understanding how the design and function of a building or public space (such as those created in Unit III) affect the neighborhoods in which they are located. In working on a particular street, students may plan to make changes by using vacant lots or razing buildings to make way for replacements. In planning their creation, they have to undertake a number of investigations regarding zoning, access, transportation, and the like. This requires trips into the neighborhood, to city hall, and elsewhere. Some students work on developing a finished street plan showing how the street will look after their plans for specific changes. Finally, students from across the four classes develop a forty-minute public production in which they display all of the artifacts—for example, models and multimedia productions—that were created during the year.

As I learned about these programs I could not help wondering about the response of inner-city potential drop-outs—some of whom showed up in Persian Gulf activities. Would they be challenged? Could they be trusted? Would anyone care to find out? It is unsettling to ponder the profligate waste of our human talent that we can tap so brilliantly only when we choose to kill adversaries. That talent could be used to heal a wounded society. But that would take a different vision.

The Perkins Act Amendments and the Dewey Tradition

In the Perkins Act Amendments, we find fascinating parallels to the debate over vocationalism at the beginning of the century. At the very end of the Perkins Act Amendments, a recommendation was included once again to send a commission to Germany to study its programs of efficient vocational training. The motivation for studying German vocational education appeared to be similar to the goal of the National Association of Manufacturers in the early 1900s: to copy the German system. However, the main thrust of the Perkins Act Amendments was to urge the development of integrated occupational/liberal studies programs like those of MIT or the Rindge School of Technical Arts—programs that could be seen as models for restructuring *general* secondary education.

This second path of integrated study for all American youth is hauntingly similar to the vision John Dewey projected prior to Smith-Hughes—an idea that was abandoned at the time. The MIT and Rindge School programs may be seen as efforts to create learning experiences that provide insights, concepts, and styles of learning that prepare young people for postindustrial living. We gain a deeper understanding, however, if we relate them to the kind of thinking Dewey was doing when he argued that "profound philosophical issues focus on the proper place and function of vocational factors in education."[27]

Two aspects of Dewey's thinking are relevant here: his resistance to the dual Taylorist divisions—in industry between

working people and the captains of industry, in schooling
between narrow, vocational skill training and education—
and his argument that education *through* the human occupations, which combine conceptualizing and executing, is the
most effective way to provide liberalizing learning—the kind
that yields insights about the effects of scientific discovery on
transforming human experience on the planet.

The publication of Thorstein Veblen's *Theory of the
Leisure Class* (1899) gave Dewey the language for stating his
sociophilosophical rejection of German-style vocationalism—
and why it was at odds with the promise of democracy.
Shortly after reading Veblen, he wrote that philosophical dual-
isms are "a survival from a dualistic past—from a society
which was dualistic practically and politically, drawing fixed
lines between classes, and dualistic intellectually."[28]

As a philosopher of the back to the people movement,
Dewey held that social democracy means abandonment of
this dualist heritage: "It means a common heritage, a common work, and a common destiny. It is flat hostility to the
ethics of modern life to suppose that there are two different
ends of life located on different planes; that the few who are
educated are to live on a plane of exclusive and isolated culture, while the many toil below on the level of practical
endeavor directed at material commodity."[29] The task he chose
for himself was to define the grounds for a social and an
educational alternative to a class-divided society.

As America entered the twentieth century, Dewey cited
the inventiveness of science and technology as the underlying
source of an industrial, corporate, enormously productive, economic order. He also saw science as an exemplar of the capacity of all humans to tap levels of creativity that had been
repressed by the social and intellectual features of feudalism.
Science and technology, by lifting the ancient curse of scarcity,
could for the first time offer a genuine opportunity to realize
the promise of the democratic vision: to open to the people at
large the possibility of personal and social fulfillment.

But the facts showed a betrayal of this hope. Dewey
came to argue that the key to understanding the betrayal lay

in realizing that the genie of science could point in two directions. Veblen's insights helped him see that science could either be turned into a servant of the materialist impulses of the "leisure classes," with competitive emulation by the middle and working classes, or, with proper analysis, it could be seen as the source of philosophy and practice that could serve the values of a social democracy. Dewey repeatedly analyzed the nature of the missed opportunity and its consequences. In his *Ethics*, Dewey deplored the perversion of science to the crass aims of the leisured classes: "Applied science works powerfully upon society, but not so much as application of science as of the mechanism of pecuniary profit, to which science itself is subordinated."[30]

On the eve of the Depression, in *The Public and Its Problems* (1927), Dewey stated that a science attached to the greed and power motive of the industrial revolution, instead of making a contribution to people's ability to control affairs for their own growth, has often contributed to the weakening of community and to an increase of human oppression. It has "played its part in generating enslavement of men, women, and children in factories in which they are animated machines to tend inanimate machines. It has maintained sordid slums, flurried and discontented careers, grinding poverty and luxurious wealth, brutal exploitation of nature and man in times of peace, and high explosives and noxious gases in times of war. Man, a child in understanding of himself, has placed in his hands physical tools of incalculable power. He plays with them like a child, and whether they work harm or good is largely a matter of accident."[31] To glorify the idea of "pure" science under such conditions, Dewey said, is an escapist rationalization.

In *Individualism Old and New*, Dewey spoke about a value cleavage in American life. The democratic theory teaches that self-respecting people can design machines for their own human and moral purposes, and religious teachings frown on a creed of self-indulgence. But "anthropologically speaking we are living in a money culture,"[32] where worth is measured by ability to get ahead materially in a competitive race that pits all against all.

The corrosive effects of materialism were being felt in all institutions including the schools. The aim of schooling, said Dewey, was being narrowed to "getting on" in the world—with growing pressure to teach utilitarian skills of making a living to suit the hierarchical skill needs of industry. Furthermore, the new "science of education," co-opted by an industrial philosophy of social efficiency, was reducing learning to the measurable content of expert-designed tests. "The school," observed Dewey, "like other agencies, has been laid hold of by strong minorities and used to subserve their own needs."[33]

As we noted in Chapter Nine, Dewey denied that the perversion of science was inherent in science itself. On the contrary, he argued that the evolutionary emergence of the community of scientific inquiries operated as a model of effective learning and democratic values. To be engaged in inquiry demanded respect for the democratic values of individuality, divergent thinking, and dialogical community. These values opened new possibilities for humans to grow in insight, meaning, and experience. For "good work" to happen in institutions being transformed by science/technology required participants with an "industrial intelligence"—a model of learning and inquiring that would enable them to understand the processes as well as the technical and social skills required at the work site. Beyond that, worker-citizens needed the capacity to weigh the effects of industrial policies on their own lives and the life of their society. They needed to make moral judgments.

After reflecting on how the city of Chicago and its schools were being shaped by a perverted form of factory industrialism, Dewey decided to open his own Laboratory School at the University of Chicago. He made the occupations the integrating core of the entire curriculum. There are clear parallels here to the kind of thinking we found in the MIT and Rindge School curricula.

What are the "occupations" for a liberalizing educational reform? This peculiar idea needs some explanation. Dewey founded the University Primary School in 1896 as a reaction against the factory-type urban schools that were being guided by the efficiency movement. In later reflections on the school in the 1930s, he said: "The controlling aim of the school . . . was to utilize the methods by which mankind has collectively and progressively advanced in skill, understanding and associated life."[34] As we have seen, for Dewey this method was represented in the work of scientific thinkers who bring to bear critical reflection and experimentation on efforts to solve problems and thereby advance understanding and knowledge. Thus Dewey insisted that the school be seen as a community of inquirers, young and old, who learned through active social processes and participation.

Influenced no doubt by the pioneering ideas on the nature of mind and self advanced by his colleague George Herbert Mead, Dewey explained that the school was designed to be a community because minds and selves are formed best by free interaction with others—through communication, cooperation, and inquiry. This was a conscious departure from an image of school as a place where lessons are to be recited. Several other principles were basic to the school's design. One was a recognition that modern urban life is too complex for a child to understand and the amount of knowledge is overwhelming. To help children, study should be organized around a framework of concepts that bring order out of the chaos. A second goal was to overcome the debilitating effects of classroom isolation. Curriculum strategies were created to establish continuity between school and the world beyond. Finally, the school should represent in the quality of its life a way of learning that demonstrates values of the democratic ideal.

Dewey hit on two interrelated ideas to establish the school dynamics he sought. One was that the conceptual axis of the course of study was to be "the development of civilization." The other was that the central pedagogical strategy was to be "through the study of occupations." Having children get a sense of the historical evolution of human civilization would enable them to comprehend the busy scientific/technical/industrial change swirling around them. The hunch was that a study of the basic human occupations could provide a framework for attaining the big perspective: occupations like the securing of basic needs of food, clothing, shelter, transportation, communications. Influenced by emerging anthropological studies, Dewey's school led students to see the effects on human experience of major economic/work-life shifts—for example, the shifts from hunting and gathering to pastoral and then to agricultural life—and, finally, how modern industrial life emerged with the scientific/technological revolutions. Children could be led to explore the consequences on the whole web of human life with each of these major cultural changes. They could examine, for instance, how the concepts and practices of work, the arts, religion, warfare, political life, and the role of women underwent changes.

In the study of clothing, the school's Chicago children, who normally purchased sweaters at the new department stores, would be given a chance to handle raw wool which they then carded, spun into thread, and wove into woolen. They could see the underlying connection between the mechanized processes in Chicago factories and the underlying handicraft processes used by their European ancestors. They could get a sense of the difference in work life of their rural forebears and the factory operators of 1900. They could reflect on the gains and losses. They could bring some order out of the booming, buzzing confusion.

Dewey saw several pedagogical justifications for using the study of occupations as the means for achieving insight into the evolution of civilization. First, occupations offered opportunities to relate school learning to out-of-school experience. They also represented "the fundamental processes and instruments by which society has made itself what it is in the subordination of nature to human ends."

Moreover, they brought into play impulses of children that are central to effective learning: the *constructive*, which moves from simple physical coordination to the use of tools and technical skills; the *investigative* and *experimental;* and the *social* and *expressive,* which involve sharing and communicating. Being occupied with an occupation maintains a balance between the intellectual and the practical. It involves continual observation of materials and continued planning and reflection in order to secure the end-in-view. In Dewey's words: "It differs from a trade because its end is . . . in the growth that comes from the continual interplay of ideas and their embodiment in action, not in external utility."[35]

Finally, the occupations were justified only if they became a means for securing a deeper liberal educational experience:

> In educational terms this means that these occupations shall not be mere practical devices . . . but active centers of scientific insight into natural materials and processes, points of departure whence children shall be led out into a realization of the historic development of man.
>
> The occupation supplies the child with genuine motive; it gives him experience at first hand; it brings him into contact with realities. It does all this but in addition it is liberalized throughout by translation into its historic and social values and scientific equivalencies. . . . [It] becomes more and more a medium, an organ of understanding—and is thereby transformed.[36]

In the Dewey elementary school, the occupations were supplemented by three academic strands: history, science, and communication and expression. I have described the nature of the school at length in *John Dewey as Educator*.

Dewey perceived the occupations, then, in the broad sense as those activities that occupy men and women in coping with life. Education *through* the occupations meant for Dewey an education that engages the intellect in reflection upon actual practical activity—the shared practices of the community that are the roots of human learning. In *Democracy and Education*, he summarized the pedagogical case for the occupations:

> The essentials of method are therefore identical
> with the essentials of reflection. They are first,
> that the pupil have a genuine situation of expe-
> rience—that there be a continuous activity in
> which he is interested for its own sake; secondly,
> that a genuine problem develop within this situ-
> ation as a stimulus to thought; third, that he pos-
> sess the information and make observations to
> deal with it; fourth, that suggested solutions
> occur to him which he shall be responsible for
> developing . . . fifth, that he have opportunity
> and occasion to test his ideas by application, to
> make their meaning clear and discover . . . their
> validity.[37]

The reader will recognize the connection between Dewey's statement about these "elements of reflection" and the rudiments of scientific method: "elements and values," which Dewey argued were necessary for all citizens of a democratic society in an age of industrialism.

As the century opened, Dewey had a vision that the power of science and technology had the potential for extending democratic and humane values. The majority of people could be freed from the age-old drudgery of physical toil. Their dignity as learners would be acknowledged as they became members of communities of inquiry in work and education. They could learn the knowledge and skills that would enable them to face change with insight and understanding. In reality, corporate industrialism became marked by bureaucratic, manipulative controls—directed by what Vaclav Havel calls the impersonal power of "systems, *apparat,* bureaucracy, artificial languages."[38]

By the end of the century, a dynamic, electronic, post-industrial reality requires some of the institutional qualities and styles of learning that Dewey spoke of. Developments like the Carl D. Perkins Vocational and Applied Technology Education Act Amendments of 1990, the MIT Integrated Studies Program, and the Rindge School's "Creating Cambridge" curriculum suggest that fresh ideas for educating the young for the world's work, ideas that incorporate features of Dewey's vision, are possible. The unanswered question is whether educational policymakers will see anything of compelling relevance in them.

Twelve

Education and Work
in the Year 2000:
Capitalism with a Human Face?

The important thing to remember is that if one works well in a potato field, the potatoes will grow. If one works well with men, they will grow. That's reality. The rest is smoke.

—Danilo Dolce (1986)

When man truly enters the age of science he will abandon his crude and destructive efforts to conquer nature. He will instead learn to insert himself into the environment in such a manner that his ways of life and technologies make him once more in harmony with nature.

—René Dubos (1972)

We learn from Robert Reich in *The Work of Nations: Preparing Ourselves for 21st Century Capitalism* that the 1950s model of industrial mass production is moving toward dinosaurian obsolescence. He makes the case that new skills for work and learning are now required—the skills of symbolic analysis. They include:

- Abstraction—the capacity to order and make meaning of the massive flow of information
- System thinking—the capacity to see the parts in relation to the whole to discover why problems arise and how components are linked together
- Experimental inquiry—the capacity to set up procedures to test and evaluate alternative ideas
- Collaboration—the need for active communication to get a variety of perspectives, as well as the capacity to create consensus when that is necessary

185

Reflection on this list shows that it requires a radical shift in our way of looking at the world and ourselves.

The mass-production industrial world was organized around a view that was linear, atomistic, hierarchical, manipulative, dualistic. The symbolic-analysis perspective, by contrast, is more contextual/ecological. It asks us to see systems in terms of the interconnectedness of the parts and their functioning and to see that the health of the whole is affected by the health of the parts and the quality of their relatedness. It requires of us a capacity to construct meaning and bring order to the way we see the functioning of the system—to be participants in meeting problems and devising change and innovation. This is quite different from a style where order is imposed on the system from above.

These skills coincide with the processes Shoshanna Zuboff describes as necessary for an informating work environment. They are congruent with many features of the restructuring movement in schooling: trends toward decentralizing, strengthening teacher autonomy at the local school level, and giving priority to active, constructivist styles of learning for children. They are skills ignored by and large by the mass-industrial style of organizing work and learning.

Reich's argument about the basic skills now needed in schooling and industry is persuasive. Before ending, I think it is important to consider two larger issues flowing from Reich's analysis—issues that go beyond the practical details involved in restructuring schools and industry: the need to make a shift in our worldviews and self-image and the implications of Reich's analysis for a democratic vision of America under electronic-era postindustrialism.

The Shift in Worldview

I was helped to see the deeper issues through my good fortune in meeting Philip G. Herbst at the Norwegian Work Research Institutes in Trondheim, Norway. Herbst was one of the pioneers in creating the democratic sociotechnical work theory referred to in Chapter Three. He and his colleagues challenged what they call "the technological fix fallacy" of classic scientific management: the assumption that all problems lend themselves to technical solutions by experts who stand outside the system. They insist that the mainstream industrial model ignores, or debases, the "socio" dimension—the capacities for the communicative, reflective, collaborative interactions of people at work. Herbst argues that new work and learning that combine high technology with high-quality human involvement could be a leading edge toward a more viable social order. We need to see, he says, that we face a choice of worldviews, and a choice of images of ourselves, in confronting the task of restructuring work and schooling.

As Herbst sees it, the significant challenges in the industrial era concerned coping with the physical environment. At this stage, life is seen as people fighting against their environment. The locus of problems lies in the physical environment, which people can understand scientifically in order to subdue it. The fundamental characteristic of this environment is that it is seen as a cluster of elements. This is the model upon which classical science built its theories of universal deterministic laws. In this world, our predominant relationship is not to ourselves but to the world of external objects. Armed with the tools of science to conquer the environment, we stand apart from it and against it. This posture results in a basic contradiction: "In the active mode, standing god-like outside the world, man controls, masters, and subjugates the environment. In the passive mode it is the environment that shapes, governs, and determines his behavior."[1]

The orientation of a science that is atomistic, mechanistic, and deterministic, one that permits mastery of the environment, also furnishes the conceptual foundation for the creation of bureaucratic organizations based on the principle of "redundancy of parts." The classic organizational design to secure productivity assumes a system of uniform replaceable parts. When "fixing" is needed, one turns to the engineering expert who provides the thinking required "to restore efficiency." The pathology of this engineer's model emerges, Herbst wryly observes, "when man begins to treat man as part of the physical environment. In the active mode, he perceives and masters others as subjects. In the passive mode, he experiences himself as object, as a cog in the machinery."[2]

In the late industrial stage, the solidity of the "modernist" model is called into question: The source of challenge comes from a fundamental change in the relationship of people to their environment. The environment, once confidently brought under scientific control, is marked now by new orders of turbulence. Moreover, the organizational patterns designed to increase control are themselves increasingly marked by unruly complexity, size, and dysfunctional change that become increasingly repugnant and unacceptable to humans.

The symptoms of breakdown appear both in the work world of the adults and in the school world of youth and their teachers. Those who cling to notions of technocratic ideology assume that the only way to "fix" the turbulence is to step up control of the parts. The possibility that the expertise itself may be the source of escalating the turbulence seems beyond comprehension.

Herbst suggests that the predominant issue in a *post*-industrial era centers on "the dense interdependent ecology of life on this globe. . . . There is no outside to man's world. The existential loneliness of humanity is not overcome by space flights. Man takes his environment along wherever he goes. The system has taken the environment into itself. Each part has the rest of the system as its environment and each part is the environment for others."[3]

What has receded, Herbst says, is the *independent physicalist type environment*, "which could be conceptualized as an aggregate or cluster of elements and which provided the basis for the immutable laws of classical science." These laws have not ceased to operate insofar as they are valid, but they no longer provide the conceptual base for understanding the problems of the present unsettled environment. "This," says Herbst, "is because the behavior of man, the relationship of man to man, and the social ecologies that have come into being do not conform to the universal and immutable principles of classical science."[4] The ability to deal successfully with this order of change depends now on building a learning capacity, a value-choosing capacity, into the system itself.

The traditional hierarchical style, based on the separation of doing, planning, and deciding, becomes increasingly inappropriate and is replaced by work groups in which these functions are integrated. "The members of these groups," says Herbst, "will to an increasing degree be able to participate in policy decisions and be capable of using specialists as consultants."[5] The shift, then, is from a feeling of alienation to a feeling of autonomy.

Herbst's model of a possible postindustrial world sees the emergence of such organizational qualities foreshadowing and supporting more general social changes. In shifts to a postindustrial world, freeing the worker's intelligence to cope with rapid change introduces an essentially new factor—the potential for *technological choice* within the organization. Herbst's experience in Norway's industrial democracy projects has led him to believe that people at work can design technologies and social relations to meet technological change and create a more satisfying quality of democratic social living:

> The critical condition for gaining control over social change in industry and society as a whole becomes, then, that we utilize the option of technological choice. To the extent that the choice of future technologies is directly correlated with social and educational changes over the same period, stability and directionality of societal development can be achieved. This is a necessary but not sufficient condition. Man has become able to create his future society, not as he has done so far, blindly and unknowingly, but within limits, consciously. What he is faced with is the problem of deciding what kind of future he wants.[6]

If a world model more conducive to well-being is to emerge, the key problem lies in *what goals* to achieve. Values and ethics become the central concern. And the means must be congruent with the ends.

From this perspective, sociotechnical theory may be seen as an alternative mode of thinking to replace the "atomistic, aggregate" orientation of an ailing mass industrialism. It abandons mechanistic assumptions about nature and production for a more ecological view of the world. It moves toward a model of integral efficiency that assumes we have to learn to produce efficiently while optimizing human values. It moves toward concepts of production that capitalize on distinctive human capacities to see the relation of parts to the whole, to communicate effectively in coping with problems, and to tap personal/subjective dimensions of learning instead of only the abstract/rational.

A forerunner of such work may be seen in certain high-tech processes where a small number of well-educated workers must respond to random, unpredictable developments. Intellectual involvement, learning communication, and commitment increasingly concentrate in primary groups where thinking and acting are integrated. People who are "left out" or who are "out of it" become a threat to the well-being of the activity. Therefore the essential question becomes: How can we sustain involvement of the whole range of human capacities of everyone in the system?

Education for a High Democratic Society?
Or Something Else?

Beyond citing the symbolic-analytic skills demanded in emerging international "high-value enterprises," Reich also assesses the American capacity for competing in the global market. Education and the ability to learn are the critical ingredients. This is so because the key assets of high-value enterprise are not so much routine labor or capital but the skills involved in linking solutions to particular needs. Reich holds that in high-value enterprise only one asset grows more valuable as it is used: the capacity for problem-identifying, problem-solving, and brokering skills. "Unlike machinery that gradually wears out," Reich observes, "raw materials that become depleted, patents and copyrights that grow obsolete, and trademarks that lose their ability to comfort, the skills and insights that come from discovering new linkages between technologies and needs actually increase with practice."[7] With human capital, people learn through practice, and the value of what they do increases as they gain experience. As Reich notes: "People fortunate enough to have had an excellent education followed by on-the-job experience doing complex things can become steadily more valuable over time."[8]

If we look with Reich at how American schools are doing to produce these symbolic-analytic skills, we find some aspects reassuring and others deeply disturbing. About 20 percent of American jobs are in the symbolic-analysis category— a substantial increase since 1950. About that percentage of America's young are being well prepared for a lifetime of symbolic-analytic work. They come from the families who send their children to private or well-furbished suburban high schools, followed by training in American colleges and universities that are the best in the world.

For the other 80 percent, the picture is different. At the low end there are American children who get almost no education or a very poor one. In the sick, impoverished urban ghettos, 40 to 50 percent of children of color do not finish high school. A similar educational fate befalls white children and children of migratory workers in rural poverty areas. Fully 17 percent of American seventeen-year-olds are functionally illiterate.[9] In the new world market, this sector of our youth, cut off from the life of the mind, is at risk of becoming permanently obsolete before they begin work. For the rest, the quality of education can vary widely—from schools that are creative, effective, and nurturing to many that offer uninspiring standardized instruction where ground is covered instead of ideas.

There is a growing dualism between the quality of education received by the upper 20 percent of American children and the rest. This tendency in education reflects a widening income discrepancy in the society at large. The deepening division is, to some extent, a product of the impact of electronic technology on work. The level of worker income depends significantly on the value placed on the skills needed in the world market. There is more demand for some skills and less for others:

> Regardless of how your job is officially classified (manufacturing, service, managerial, technical, secretarial, and so on), or the industry in which you work (automotive, steel, computer, advertising, finance, food processing), your real competitive position in the world economy is coming to depend on the function you perform in it. Herein lies the real reason why incomes are diverging. The fortunes of routine producers are declining. In-person servers are also becoming poorer, although their fates are less clear cut. But symbolic analysts—who solve, identify, and broker new problems—are, by and large, succeeding in the world economy.[10]

At mid-century, when we were at our peak, the economic fortunes of many Americans tended to rise or fall depending on whether the giant pyramidal corporations they worked for prospered or languished. Since then, many of these industries have steadily been losing ground. Because of the dramatic improvements in worldwide communications and transportation technologies, the core national corporations are being replaced by international corporate webs that can increase profits by imaginative problem-solving and brokering. Designs, instructions, advice, visual symbols—all can be communicated precisely and at ever lower costs anywhere in the world. New state-of-the-art machinery can be installed wherever it is profitable. A result, Reich says, is that instead of all boats rising or falling with the economic tide, Americans tend to find themselves in three different boats: Those with the symbolic-analytic skills are rising; those with routine production skills are sinking; those with in-person skills are sinking, too, but at a slower pace.

The world's population increases at 12,000 per hour. Millions of impoverished people are eager to work for a small fraction of the wages of American routine producers. Increasingly electronic-guided technology can be shipped overseas— "out-sourced" to give Third Worlders work that used to remain in the states. Laborsaving computer technology is also cutting into many person-server jobs; witness automatic car washes, automated tellers, self-serve gas pumps. Other technologies, of course, produce new jobs, but intense competition is tending to keep wages low.

One of the results is a dramatic shift in the distribution of incomes—a shift that accelerated in the 1980s. Some Americans are doing well in the global economy, some are falling behind. The trend toward greater inequality, plotted by Bennett Harrison and Barry Bluestone in *The Great U Turn,* has since been confirmed by congressional studies. Between 1977 and 1990, for example, the average income of the poorest fifth of American families declined by about 7 percent while the average income of the richest fifth of American families increased about 15 percent. By 1990, the richest fifth of Americans received over half of the nation's income, with the top 5 percent getting 26 percent—all-time records in both instances. Meanwhile, the average income of the poorest fifth of Americans in 1990 was 3.7 percent of the nation's total income, down from 5.5 percent in 1970. This trend was reported in Western Europe, as well, but not nearly so pronounced.[11]

Many complex factors are involved here, but one new trend is striking: the increase in the number of the *working* poor who fall below the poverty level. Between 1978 and 1987, the number of *working* Americans who fell below the poverty level rose by nearly 2 million, or 2.3 percent. Within this group, the number of full-time, year-round workers who fell below the poverty level rose even more sharply—by 43 percent.

The gap widened even within the core American corporations (those formally owned and operated by Americans).

By 1990, the average hourly earnings (adjusted for inflation) of nonsupervisory workers were lower than any year since 1965. But the salaries of top executives, and their advisers and consultants, rose to unimaginable heights. Between 1977 and 1990, the average earnings of America's top executives rose by 220 percent—not counting perquisites like company cars and planes and country club memberships. In Japan, compensation of major CEOs is 17 times that of the average worker; in France and Germany, 23 to 25 times; in Britain, 35 times; in America, roughly 160 times. A couple of examples illustrate the point. In March 1990, Chrysler announced that its profits had dropped 81 percent while its CEO, Lee Iaccoca, was given a 25 percent salary increase to $4.6 million. In 1990, troubled General Dynamics posted a loss of $577 million and in 1991 laid off 35,000 workers. Yet the top twenty-five executives got bonuses equal to their annual salaries, and William Anders, the CEO, after one year with the company, received a $500,000 bonus in cash and stock worth $532,978.[12] With this example of corporate accountability before them, teachers have a right to be puzzled by insistence from the business community that their chief obligation is to be accountable in terms of bottom-line numbers.

Another significant development was the clear connection between the widening income gap and the level of education. Between 1973 and 1987, the earnings of workers with only a high school certificate declined by 12 percent (and among blacks by 44 percent). For those who were high school dropouts, inflation-adjusted earnings fell by an additional 18 percent. Meanwhile, male graduates of four-year colleges in the same period came out somewhat ahead of the game—earnings of $50,115 in 1987 as compared to $49,531 in 1973. But the gap between college graduates and their high school counterparts widened dramatically. In 1980, the typical college graduate earned 80 percent more than the high school graduate; by 1990 the gap had nearly doubled. Reich's conclusion from such statistics is that people's income relates to their level of education: "If you graduated from college, your earnings improved; if you did not and especially if you were male, you get poorer."[13] The basic cause is rooted in the different functions people are coming to perform within the global economy.

As America enters the 1990s it is not surprising to find the social divisions of the society paralleled by a similar division in the kind of education American children are experiencing. The children of those who were working in the symbolic-analysis sector of the economy were getting an education in well-financed private or suburban schools that taught the core symbolic-analytic skills and attitudes: abstraction, system thinking, experimentation, and collaboration. They were at work in well-equipped school settings, in classes with low teacher-student ratios, taught by committed teachers who had enough autonomy to project their creative ideas into the job of teaching. For them teaching was a profession. They were not limited by prescribed content and tests. Their students, after intellectual engagement with their studies and the help of a few days of exam preparation, did well on the tests. They were ready for advanced study in America's fine universities.

What about the rest? While many good things were going on in the mainstream school system, it continued to be strongly influenced by the factory school tradition created in the early 1990s. In the early decades of the century, America was going full blast in creating a powerful, mass production factory system. There was a strong growth of higher education as more and more upper-echelon managers, engineers, and technical experts needed university training. At the other end, the main prerequisite for most routinized factory jobs was the ability to understand written and oral directives, to do basic arithmetic, and to have sufficient self-control to follow the directives of central authorities.

As industrialism and urbanism advanced, hordes of children who no longer had early access to apprenticeship, or work on the family farm, needed access to schooling. It took an enormous effort to build the factorylike schools to house these children and figure out what to do with them after they arrived. Ellwood P. Cubberley, dean of the School of Education

at Stanford, described the kind of schools that hurriedly were
being created:

> Our schools are, in a sense, factories in which
> the raw materials are to be shaped and fashioned
> into products to meet the various demands of life.
> The specifications for manufacturing come from
> the demands of the twentieth century civilization,
> and it is the business of the school to build its
> pupils to the specifications laid down. This
> demands good tools, specialized machinery, con-
> tinuous measurement of production to see if it is
> according to specifications, [and] the elimination
> of waste in manufacture.[14]

This system, expanded and elaborated, was the one in
place when America was at its industrial peak at mid-century.
Children moved from grade to grade through a preplanned
sequence of subjects organized around basal texts. Those students with the best capacity to absorb the facts and accept the
routine were placed on fast tracks that could lead to higher
things. The rest were sorted into average or slow sections.
Standardized tests coordinated with standardized content were
regularly administered. As in the adult workplaces, discipline
and order were prized above all. Teachers, like the workers in
mass production, had little discretion over what they did.
They were required to follow plans and use materials designed by specialists at the highest level of the educational
hierarchy and transmitted through layers of administrators
and supervisors. The system loaned itself to economy of size
in large standardized buildings. The standardized "egg-crate"
structure was challenged periodically by efforts at reform, progressive or otherwise, but had a remarkable resilience for ward-
ing off change.

While there is truth in this picture, it is an overgeneral-
ization. Good things happened for many children whose
desire to learn and grow was sparked by dedicated, heroic
teachers. But by 1990 there was a disgraceful level of decay in

the physical plants of impoverished urban schools. As Deborah Meier put it: "The physical condition of New York City schools is simply an outrage. There's no way to have good education in terribly overcrowded schools, where classes are being held in hallways and gyms, where the bathrooms don't work and the ceilings are falling in. It's a delusion to think that these things don't matter—that you can teach well in any setting."[15] Cant about raising scores in such schools by national standardized tests and voucher plans, and rhetoric about making American children Number One in the world in math and science, while at the same time avoiding the true financial investment required to get serious, is a hollow mockery.

Two Visions of Tomorrow

As we enter the 1990s we see then an America at a critical juncture: How will it organize itself for engagement in the electronic, global market? How will it define itself as a democracy under postindustrialism?

A critical component for success, both national and personal, is access to a thorough education permeated with symbolic-analytic skills and values. Clearly there is a growing gap between the fifth of American children getting that kind of education and the rest. By the end of the 1980s, as the gap widened, one in four American children under the age of three lived in families below the poverty level: 44 percent of all black children, 36 percent of Hispanics, and 15 percent of whites.[16]

In response to such dualism, we face a choice between two general courses of action: The first course assumes that we can hold steady on the present course with some not-too-expensive patching of American schooling to improve our position. The assumption is that with the present cadre of symbolic analysts and a work force sufficiently trained in "the basics" we can design and administer high technology to nicely hold our own. Those at the higher and middle levels can be counted on to turn their eyes away from the growing

segregation of Americans by income and ignore the embar-
rassing social disarray at the bottom. The second option
would require a major shift in the nation's priorities. A decision would be made to counter the growing income and educational division by framing and adopting policies to assure
that all American children, regardless of class or race, would
be given opportunities to learn symbolic-analytic skills. All
would have the chance to become viable in meeting the
demands of the global market. All would have the chance to
become responsible participants in the demanding postindustrial institutions in the making. This option would require a
commitment by the presently favored sector of American
society to make resources, ideas, and leadership available to
everybody.

The first course is the one we are now on—and, frankly,
likely to stay on. To choose it is to choose a society wounded
by class and learning divisions. For the near future, it probably can be made to work. The symbolic-analysis sector is well
equipped to flourish in the global market, and our educational system is well prepared to replenish it. The way to
keep it functioning is by the automating option. This high-
tech elite may see their society handicapped by an impoverished nonwhite sector, largely "out of it," and many workers
equipped only with mediocre education and training. But
they can live with it. They can choose the high-tech, centrally
administered, automating option to keep America in the competitive race. Computer-driven equipment can be installed
overseas and designed to function with moderately skilled
low-wage workers led by a few highly trained technicians. At
home, accepting the reality of a work force only partially
educated by standardized schooling, the elite can again adopt
the automating option—in other words, get by with the
design of automated high-tech equipment under centralized
managerial control—and avoid the informating option, which
reduces hierarchy and increases effectiveness but demands a
major revisioning of American work and education.

This option reduces the democratic vision to a narrow
social Darwinism. It sorts out the fittest and provides oppor-

tunities for the ablest among the lesser. It is based on the bet that the middle and lower middle classes can be kept in line by an adequate standard of living, by the diversions of consumerism, and by playing on racial fears. The social divisiveness, however, could become increasingly troublesome. Extrapolations about the future are risky, but one can project a not-too-far-fetched scenario.

By 2020, the top fifth of American earners will earn more than 60 percent of American income, with the bottom fifth dropping to 2 percent.[17] The high-tech elite will withdraw further into their secure enclaves, living a life with excellent health care, challenging work, effective schools, and global travel and linkages. They can tolerate the disorder beyond the pale by walling themselves off, both physically and psychologically, from those who have been left out. Moreover, one might expect more moves toward a security state with investment in electronically equipped security forces, more high-security prisons, and a stepping up of executions for those who have truly "stepped over the line." There will be less contact between these enclaves and the rest of society. The urban and rural poor will live largely out of sight in their own decaying sectors. The despair and hopelessness of their children will be a fact of life—as will be the human warehousing of thousands of minority youth in prisons.

We may choose that way. It is not a vision of America as "a light on the hill" to the rest of the world's burgeoning and impoverished population. But it is not our only choice. We could be guided by another vision—one that Lynn White in *Dynamo and Virgin Reconsidered* refers to as a "high democratic culture"—one in which the concern for human values and excellence of aristocratic traditions would be combined with the democratic concern for the dignity of each and the desire to include all in meaningful participation.[18]

Such a culture would require a recognition by America's leaders that a dangerously divided society, in the long run, is an intolerable threat to the country's moral and material well-being and survival. It would require a decision to take the power of new technology and combine it with the values of our democratic tradition. It would require recognition that the best bet for America's social well-being is a population equipped across the board with symbolic-analytic skills tempered by ecological awareness and deep appreciation for the values and traditions of democracy. Where work is concerned, it would require a commitment to seize the advantage of having thoroughly educated workers to create environments that would combine high tech with high worker involvement—the informating style.

There is no more dramatic example of this present class-riven society than the physical features of American work and schooling in the heart of the U.S. financial capital: the island of Manhattan. The sumptuous corporate towers, loaded with ever-changing electronics that link the inhabitants to their counterparts anywhere in the world, shout the message that America is a world-class economic power. Compare that image with the condition of the public schools on that same island. The reality of the new economic world-in-the-making asserts that sustaining a world-class economic power depends on the creation of world-class schooling. Do we have the imagination to envision the features of world-class schools for all the children of Manhattan? And having created the conception, would there be a commitment to create the schools—not only in New York but across the country?

To create a society of world-class schools for a world-class economy would demand a dramatic change in priorities. It would demand an investment in education, at all levels, of the order employed in building a high-tech military machine during the Cold War. Just the sheer cost of razing the decayed shells of inner-city school buildings and replacing them with modern centers to support symbolic-analytic learning would itself be enormous. A decision would be needed to create exciting learning centers with physical accoutrements comparable to those of American corporations—with readily available computer facilities for all students and teachers, fine laboratories for the sciences, the arts, and language instruction, and, difficult to imagine, air conditioning. Such schools, led by leaders committed to the new vision, would attract to teaching some of our most able and imaginative young adults. The real test of progress will be to count how many inner-city schools have been turned into such world-class learning communities by the year 2000.

If this image of a new quality of schooling for American children seems mere fantasy, it demonstrates how far we are from getting serious about the educational resources we need. We cannot get the education we require to be competitive in a high-tech postindustrialism, and to tap the array of strengths of our democratic culture, without a major federal financial commitment. Once we face that fact squarely, we can see current proposals for education on-the-cheap—vouchers, national testing, and so forth—as the fainthearted evasions they are.

What would be the features of the new education? I do not have a blueprint. None of us has. The details will have to be created in the years ahead by the talented minds who are attracted to education. Some glimpses, however, of the quality needed can be obtained by reflecting on features that were appearing in the early 1990s. Central would be the creation of learning environments that support the skills of symbolic analysis—the skills essential to the functioning of the electronic global economy.

Young symbolic analysts will have learned to read, write, and calculate, of course, and will have done serious study in the humanities and sciences. The ways they learn to learn, however, will be critically important. They will certainly need the skills of calling up information on the computer. More important, they will need to learn how to conceptualize problems and solutions. They will need learning in depth to refine the basic symbolic-analytic skills: abstraction, system thinking, experimentation, and collaboration.

Since they will live in a world with an overwhelming flow of data and information, the capacity for *abstraction* will be essential—the capacity for discovering patterns and meanings; the skills to simplify a complex reality so that it can be understood and integrated to reveal new solutions, problems, and choices. Both students and teachers must be viewed from the *homo poeta* perspective: humans as meaning makers.

Related and equally essential are the skills of *system thinking*. Instead of seeing the world as made up of discrete bits of data that can be learned in isolation, system thinking involves the capacity to understand the processes by which parts of reality are linked together into wholes. With system thinking, students will be taught to examine why problems arise and how they are connected to other problems.

This skill, in turn, requires the capacity for *experimental thinking*—the skills for generating and testing hypotheses, the habit of seeing ideas as truth claims to be checked against data and experience. Many schools talk about the experimental method but rarely offer opportunities to practice it.

Then there is the capacity to *collaborate*. In the new work of symbolic analysts and in informating workplaces, problems are often confronted by creative teams—whether they are seeking a scientific discovery, dreaming up a marketing strategy, or designing an innovative product. Mutual learning occurs within the teams as insights, experiences, puzzles, and solutions are shared and pondered. The skills of communicating ideas imaginatively are honed so that other teams and individuals in the system can benefit. The symbolic-analytic mind is trained to be curious, creative, skeptical, and communicative.

I would add three skills to the four mentioned by Reich. One would be disciplined effort. In a world rent with change and the challenges that come with it, people will need disciplined commitment to marshal the courage and creativity to cope with reality. In work and schooling, we need to take responsibility for defining what is desired and required. We need the capacity for delaying immediate gratification. We need the willingness to make sustained efforts to attain the goals.

Second, we need to cultivate appreciation of the aesthetic. Ugliness in our lives diminishes us in subtle ways. We show disrespect for children and teachers when we warehouse them in huge impersonal factorylike buildings. Care about the quality of learning and work is nurtured when we create settings that are aesthetically pleasing. Similarly, we must learn the importance of tapping the resources of the intuitive—the source of creative visions. Linear, authoritarian environments stifle the capacity to contact our human intuition, which opens new ways of seeing and acting.

Finally, there is the need to cultivate the skill of weighing and making value judgments. The new world of work, to function effectively, must be built with new respect for the dignity and *quality* of life experienced by people at work in it. Concern for quality in addition to quantity must be made a concern of society and its institutions. The young must be taught how to weigh policies and actions in terms of the impact on both the natural and human environments. We are doing grave damage to the thin balance of forces that make life possible on our planet. Thanks to the power of the media, we are beginning to realize our common vulnerability. But we cannot change our ways of relating to the natural system until we change the quality of our ways of relating to ourselves. We cannot have a natural ecology without a social ecology.

Toward a Fresh Start

The formal education of most American children contains all too few of these skills. It often contains their opposites. What is to be learned is prepackaged into lesson plans, textbooks, and lectures. The obedient student is to demonstrate individual mastery by successful performance on tests coordinated with the content. Excelling over others is the way to advance. The underlying lesson is that it is someone else's responsibility to give meaning to the swirl of data and information surrounding us. The student's job is to follow orders in mastering it.

Although such models produce malleable populations, they cheat us of the strengths we need. We need a fresh start, but we do not have to begin *de novo*. Imaginative American educators throughout this century have resisted pressures to reduce learning to a standardized production function. The alternatives, however, have not been widely incorporated into the mainline system. In the early 1990s, many features of the symbolic-analysis style of learning have been incorporated into aspects of the restructuring movement. By reviewing some examples from previous chapters we may remind ourselves that Americans do not lack pioneering ideas.

In Chapter Eleven, we saw fresh ideas for integrating liberal and occupational studies that give insight into the historical evolution that eventually produced electronic post-industrialism. MIT's Integrated Studies Program involves students in study of the historical development of human occupations and combines academic study with hands-on activities. Always the effort is made to see the connection between scientific/technical innovations and the effects on cultural change.

The Rindge School's "Creating Cambridge" curriculum provides an opportunity for students to see a community as a functioning system. It involves students in constructivist learning in which they collect data on a part of the community and its needs and then pose their own ideas for solution. They communicate their findings through multimedia presentations and other means. Lighthouse Schools that function in this way would demonstrate that the teaching of symbolic-analytic skills, attitudes, and values is possible.

In the Carl D. Perkins Vocational and Applied Technology Education Act Amendments of 1990, we saw a recognition that a high school diploma is less and less viable as a terminal certificate. Groundwork has been laid to coordinate secondary studies with the high-tech skills taught in two-year community colleges. This, in turn, opens opportunities for further study throughout a person's working career.

In Chapter Ten on computers, we noted that 85 percent of computer-assisted instruction turns this technology into a mechanized workbook. The ACOT program of Apple Computer, Inc., rejects the concept of knowledge acquisition as mere accumulation of facts. ACOT designers perceive significant knowledge as *personal* knowledge that has to be constructed or discovered by the learner—and they assume that this style of learning should permeate the work of teachers as well as of students. ACOT rejected reform by external imposition of technology on pliant teacher clients. Teachers were given an opportunity to construct their own ways of integrating the power of computer technology into their ideas about teaching. Students were brought into experiments that combine collaborative learning with computer technology.

In inner-city situations, we noted in Chapter Eight James Comer's School Development Plan in New Haven, Connecticut. It offers a challenge to centralized bureaucracy by a school governance and community participation plan. Recognizing that vital changes must come from within the school community itself, Comer and colleagues established governance teams with elected parents, teachers, and mental health and child development specialists. These teams worked together to pinpoint problems and pose solutions. Within a few years, two schools with the lowest attendance and achievement records were turned into two of the district's best.

In Henry Levin's Accelerated Schools Project we saw the simple, breathtaking idea that America's children of poverty, "at-risk children," should be given the same imaginative, interactive, enriched kinds of learning that are provided for gifted children and the rich. It is an updated version of John Dewey's advice at the opening of the century—that what we wish for our own children we should wish for all children.

In one of the most impoverished parts of New York City we found a dynamic "schools of choice" program in Manhattan's District 4. In contrast to factory-like drabness, the educators and citizens of the district designed smallness within bigness by creating forty-four schools in twenty buildings. These "schools within schools" provide a wide array of program choices to meet the diverse interests and needs of the district's children. Decentralized strategies have permitted authentic involvement by teachers, parents, and students.

In Chapter Nine, we saw middle-class community involvement in the Cougar Valley Elementary School of Silverdale, Washington, lead to cooperative teams changing the school culture by state-of-the-art computer technology. In Silverdale, teachers function as teams of professionals, sharing and testing ideas about how technology can be used to manage learning and to diagnose, present, and evaluate it. We are finding that it is possible to put instructional technology to work in ways that do not simply reinforce standardized routine.

There is a pressing need for a program that would incorporate creative ACOT-style computer technology with the learning of inner-city youth—a program that would teach computer competence and symbolic-analytic skills simultaneously. Could we discover strategies that would enable properly educated youth to vault directly from the ghetto into high-tech work? Experience with minority troops in the high-tech Gulf War suggests that we would be derelict not to make the try. But we must beware the trap of thinking that this could be done in a massive, hurried, mandated way. A lesson of ACOT is that teachers need a year to overcome their insecurities about the technology. Even more important is their need for an environment that supports their efforts to relate the technology to their creativity about teaching. Mandated crash programs can kill promising ideas.

On the troublesome issue of testing, we saw this nation poised to take off in several directions: We have the technology now to create a centralized national testing system. It could be designed to provide microsecond feedback on children's test scores from any district in the country. We could pit schools, districts, and states against each other in test score competition. If that is what we want, we can get it. Certainly there will be strong pressures in favor of this idea as the guaranteed way to become Number One in the world.

But we also noted the voices warning that such a national test score race could reinforce standardization, cripple teachers' creativity, and damage the qualities of learning most needed. The Japanese, masters of Exam Hells, are sounding the same warning to themselves. We saw, in contrast, a growing number of efforts to design forms of evaluation that give priority to preserving the integrity of teaching and learning.

Throughout this account, I have avoided any suggestion that there is only one right way to go. I do think, however, that we can cite the priorities that must be honored to meet the challenges of this new age. We must then give ourselves flexibility and freedom to explore alternatives. And in exploring alternatives, there is no wiser voice we could heed than the words of John Bremer, founder of the Philadelphia Parkway School Without Walls Program: "There is no learning without structure . . . and . . . there is no learning without 'unstructure.' The function of the educator . . . is to provide the combination of order and disorder, of structure and unstructure, which will, on the one hand, support the student as he learns, and on the other hand provide him with something to learn."[19] Ignoring that principle has led to the foundering of many promising alternatives of the past.

My hunch is that we, and other countries, will have to find our way in terms of our own unique traditions. In our case, the states, with some federal coordination, will set the broad objectives. Local initiatives and networking for exchange of ideas and policies will provide the means. (The Japanese trusted the values of their tradition, and there is no reason why we cannot trust ours.)

If we decide that cultivation of symbolic-analytic skills for *all* our children is of key importance, then we must wage a vigorous fight to obtain the realistic funding to make that possible. We will be working from a new vision. It will require massive funding from the federal level as well as from traditional sources. There will be controversy and conflict because cultural values will be in conflict—values of the bureaucratic control tradition versus values from the democratic tradition, values of atomistic individualism versus values of ecological contextualism.

If concern for the democratic values emerges on top, we will have an opportunity to engage in an exciting project: the possibility that we can take our increasing cultural and racial diversity, a cross section of the world's diversity, and create a political economy and a form of education that brings high technology and democratic values into creative collaboration—a model of informating workplaces and the educational means to make them possible. A capitalism with a human face?

We would be a society striving to become a high democratic society centered on the principle articulated by Kalman H. Silvert: "A democratic political economy must begin and end with the person-in-society, seeing him as both end and means, and combining his reason and actions in empowered participation."[20]

We would be a society in which the processes of technological change would be disciplined by the political wisdom of democracy—a society in which only those technologies and social systems would be designed that match our best sense of who we are and what we want this society to be.

══════ Notes ══════

Chapter One

1. Hazel Henderson, "A New Economics," in Dyckman Vermilye, ed., *Work and Education* (San Francisco: Jossey-Bass, 1977), p. 235.
2. Vaclav Havel, *Living in Truth* (London: Faber & Faber, 1990), pp. 153–154.
3. Jo Ann Boydston, ed., *The Middle Works of John Dewey (1899–1924),* Vol. 10 (Carbondale: Southern Illinois University Press, 1980), p. 137.

Chapter Two

1. Mike Cooley, *Architect or Bee?* (Boston: South End Press, 1981), p. 100.
2. Ernest Becker, *The Structure of Evil: An Essay on the Unification of the Science of Man* (New York: Free Press, 1968).
3. Sara Freedman, Jane Jackson, and Katherine Boles, *The*

Effect of Teaching on Teachers (Bismarck: Center for Teaching and Learning, University of North Dakota, 1986). The quotations are from pages 11–20 of the study.

4. Deborah Meier, "Good Schools Are Still Possible," *Dissent,* Fall 1987, p. 546.

5. John Goodlad, *A Place Called School* (New York: McGraw-Hill, 1984), pp. 229–230.

6. Arthur Wirth, *Productive Work in Industry and Schools: Becoming Persons Again* (Lanham, Md.: University Press of America, 1983), p. 133.

7. Meier, "Good Schools," p. 544.

8. Denis Goulet, *The Uncertain Promise* (New York: IDOC/North America, 1977), p. 30.

9. Arthur Wirth, "Basal Readers—'Dominant But Dead' vs. Gadamer and Language for Hermeneutic Understanding," *Journal of Thought* 24, nos. 3 and 4 (Fall/Winter 1989): 4–19.

10. Kenneth S. Goodman and others, *Report Card on Basal Readers* (Katonak, N.Y.: Robert C. Owen, 1988), pp. iii–v, 122–131.

11. Richard J. Bernstein, *Beyond Objectivism and Relativism* (Philadelphia: University of Pennsylvania Press, 1983), p. 144.

12. *Rethinking Schools,* December/January 1988, p. 1.

13. Ibid., September/October 1987, p. 2.

14. Goodman and others, *Report Card,* p. 24.

15. Ibid., pp. 70–72.

16. Ibid., p. 67.

17. Ibid., p. 87.

18. Ibid., p. 81.

19. Ibid., p. 108.

20. *Rethinking Schools,* March/April 1987, p. 7.

21. Allan Luke, "Making 'Dick and Jane': Historical Genesis of the Modern Basal Reader," *Teachers College Record* 89, no. 1 (Fall 1987): 91–103.

22. Ibid., p. 111.

23. Edward L. Thorndike, "Measurement in Education," *Teachers College Record,* November 1921, p. 371.

24. Goodman and others, *Report Card*, pp. 33–34.

25. Ibid., p. 125.

26. Michel Foucault, *Discipline and Punish* (New York: Vintage Books, 1979), p. 222.

27. Ibid., p. 188.

28. Ibid., p. 140.

29. *The Work of Jeremy Bentham* (New York: Russell & Russell, 1962), vol. 4, p. 44.

30. Foucault, *Discipline and Punish*, p. 200.

31. Ibid., pp. 184–194 et passim.

32. Ibid., p. 186.

33. Bernstein, *Beyond Objectivism*, pp. 131–139, 155–165.

34. Hans-Georg Gadamer, *Truth and Method* (New York: Crossroad, 1986), p. 230.

35. See Bernstein, *Beyond Objectivism*, p. 150.

36. Gadamer, *Truth and Method*, p. 231.

37. Ibid., pp. 94–95, and chap. 2, "Play as the Ontological Explanation," pp. 91–108.

38. Ibid., p. 446. See also Georgia Warnke, *Gadamer* (Stanford: Stanford University Press, 1987), pp. 49–51.

39. Hans-Georg Gadamer, *Reason in the Age of Science* (Cambridge, Mass.: MIT Press, 1986), p. 124.

40. Gadamer, *Truth and Method*, p. 58.

41. Ibid., pp. 325–333.

42. Ibid., p. 238.

43. Ibid.

44. Ibid., pp. 269–273.

45. Anne Haas Dyson, "The Value of 'Time Off Task': Young Children's Spontaneous Talk and Deliberate Text," *Harvard Educational Review* 57, no. 4 (November 1987): 396–420.

46. See Warnke, *Gadamer*, p. 228.

47. *Rethinking Schools*, May/June 1988, p. 5.

48. *Rethinking Schools*, May/June 1987, p. 3.

49. Ibid., pp. 16–17.

50. See Bernstein, *Beyond Objectivism*, p. 159.

Chapter Three

1. Martin Carnoy and Henry M. Levin, *Schooling and Work in the Democratic State* (Stanford: Stanford University Press, 1985), pp. 53–56.
2. "Skills, Schools and Technology" (Stanford: Institute for Research on Educational Finance and Governance, 1985), p. 2.
3. Robert Draper, "The Golden Arm," *New York Review of Books*, October 24, 1985, pp. 46–49.
4. "The Aerospace Labor Crunch," *Newsweek*, July 18, 1988, p. 45.
5. "Management Discovers the Human Side of Automation," *Business Week*, September 29, 1986, p. 71.
6. Henry M. Levin and R. W. Rumberger, *The Educational Implications of High Technology*, Project Report No. 83–84 (Stanford: Institute for Research on Educational Finance and Governance, 1983), p. 2.
7. Ibid., pp. 4–5.
8. Thomas Bailey, *Jobs of the Future and the Skills They Will Require* (Berkeley: National Center for Research in Vocational Education, University of California, 1991).
9. Ibid., p. 15.
10. Robert B. Reich, *The Next American Frontier* (New York: New York Times Books, 1983), p. 19.
11. See Arthur G. Wirth, *Productive Work in Industry and Schools: Becoming Persons Again* (Lanham, Md.: University Press of America, 1983), chap. 2.
12. "Human Side of Automation," p. 71.
13. I have visited auto plants and talked with both union and management people. For one account, see "Where America Beats Japan," *World Monitor*, January 1991, pp. 22–25.
14. "Workers as Bosses," *St. Louis Post-Dispatch*, December 2, 1990, p. E-1.
15. Ibid.
16. Shoshanna Zuboff, *In the Age of the Smart Machine: The Future of Work and Power* (New York: Basic Books, 1988), pp. 5–9.
17. Ibid., p. 7.

Chapter Four

1. Benjamin Duke, *The Japanese School: Lessons for Industrial America* (New York: Praeger, 1986), p. 23.
2. "Bushido as an Ethical System," in *The Works of Inazo Nitobe* (Tokyo: University of Tokyo Press, 1969), vol. I, pp. 3–153. (Originally published 1900.)
3. Duke, *The Japanese School*, p. 123.
4. Ibid., p. 21.
5. Ibid., p. 228.

Chapter Five

1. Zuboff, *Age of the Smart Machine*.
2. ABC News, "Surveillance on the Job," transcript, June 23, 1987.
3. Zuboff, *Age of the Smart Machine*, pp. 62–63.
4. Ibid., p. 179.
5. Ibid., p. 63.
6. Ibid., p. 72.
7. Ibid., p. 75.
8. Ibid., p. 200.
9. Ibid., p. 357.
10. Ibid., p. 285.
11. Henderson, "A New Economics," p. 235.
12. Robert B. Reich, *The Work of Nations: Preparing Ourselves for 21st Century Capitalism* (New York: Knopf, 1991).

Chapter Six

1. K. Cooper, "Education Secretary Calls for Restructuring of Public Schools," *Center Daily Times*, State College, Pa., May 20, 1989.
2. *Investing in Our Children: Business and the Public Schools* (New York: Committee for Economic Development, 1985), p. 7.
3. Goodlad, *A Place Called School*, pp. 229–230.

Chapter Seven

1. Report of the National Commission on Testing and Public Policy, *From Gatekeeper to Gateway: Transforming Testing in America* (Chestnut Hill, Mass.: Boston College, 1990), p. 19.

2. Richard Greb, "Teacher Perfect," *Northwestern Perspective,* Fall 1989, p. 37.

3. Report of the National Commission, p. 6.

4. Ibid., pp. 14–17.

5. Ibid., p. 18.

6. Mary Lee Smith, "Put It to the Test: The Effects of External Testing on Teachers," *Educational Researcher* 20, no. 5 (June/July 1991): 10.

7. Linda Darling-Hammond, "Achieving Our Goals: Superficial or Structural Reforms?," *Phi Delta Kappan,* December 1990, p. 290.

8. Report of the National Commission, p. 5.

9. Ibid., p. 38.

10. National Commission on Children, *Beyond Rhetoric: A New American Agenda for Children and Families* (Washington, D.C.: National Commission on Children, 1991), p. 182.

11. George Madaus (interview), "New Ways of Thinking About Testing," *Phi Delta Kappan,* April 1989, p. 644.

12. *New York Times,* May 25, 1990, p. A12.

13. Report of the National Commission, pp. 9–10.

14. Ibid., pp. x–xii.

15. Seymour Sarason, *The Predictable Failure of Educational Reform* (San Francisco: Jossey-Bass, 1990), p. 8.

16. *St. Louis Post-Dispatch,* September 9, 1991, p. A-1.

17. S. Chiara, "Schools Plan: Big Goals, Little Money," *New York Times,* February 2, 1990, p. A-19.

18. Madaus, *New Ways of Thinking,* p. 645.

19. Darling-Hammond, "Achieving Our Goals," pp. 294–295.

20. Madaus, *New Ways of Thinking,* p. 645.

21. Editorial Board, "Toward Authentic Assessment," *Democracy and Education,* Fall 1990, p. 6.

22. Ibid., pp. 6-7.
23. See "What Is Authentic Evaluation?," *Democracy and Education*, Fall 1990, pp. 17-20.
24. Iris C. Rothberg, "I Never Promised You First Place," *Phi Delta Kappan*, December 1990, p. 286.
25. Linda Darling-Hammond, "Achieving Our Goals: Superficial or Structural Reforms," *Phi Delta Kappan*, December 1990, p. 296.
26. *St. Louis Post-Dispatch*, August 16, 1991, p. 10A.
27. Ibid., August 28, 1991, p. 1C.
28. Darling-Hammond, "Achieving Our Goals," pp. 294-295. Emphasis added.
29. Deborah Meier, "Bush and the Schools: A Hard Look," *Dissent*, Summer 1991, pp. 330-331.

Chapter Eight

1. Anne Lewis, *Restructuring America's Schools* (Arlington, Va.: American Association of School Administrators, 1989), p. 3.
2. Ibid., p. 7.
3. Ibid., p. 5.
4. Mary Anne Raywid, "The Evolving Effort to Improve Schools: Pseudo-Reform, Incremental Reform, and Restructuring," *Phi Delta Kappan*, October 1990, p. 142.
5. See, for example, Lewis, *Restructuring America's Schools*, pp. 158-160.
6. See Raymond J. Domenico, *Model for Choice: A Report on Manhattan's District 4* (New York: Manhattan Institute, 1989), pp. 1-26.
7. See Lewis, *Restructuring America's Schools*, pp. 156-158, and "Parent Power: Chicago Parents Struggle to Institute Radical School Reforms," *Rethinking Schools*, March/April 1990, pp. 10-12.
8. *Education That Works: An Action Plan for the Education of Minorities* (Cambridge, Mass.: Quality Education for Minorities Program, Massachusetts Institute of Technology, 1990).

9. Ibid., p. 45.
10. Ibid., p. 47.
11. Ibid., p. 46.
12. Dennis W. Cheek and Leonard J. Waks, *Technological Literacy IV: Proceedings of the Fourth National Technological Literacy Conference,* Arlington, Va., February 3–5, 1989, p. 425.
13. *Education That Works,* pp. 49–54.
14. Ibid., p. 50.
15. My account of the Accelerated Schools Project is based on papers available from Accelerated Schools Project, 402 S (CERAS), Stanford University, Stanford, CA 94305-3084. I have interviewed teachers in such programs in the St. Louis area. See also Henry M. Levin, "Accelerated Schools: A New Strategy for At Risk Students" and "At Risk Students in a Yuppie Age," *Educational Policy* 4 (4) (1990): 283–295; two articles in *Accelerated Schools,* "What Are Accelerated Schools?" (Winter 1991), and "Getting Started" (Spring 1991); and Laurel Shaper Walters, "Students Take the Fast Track," *Christian Science Monitor,* December 19, 1990 (reprint).
16. Henry M. Levin, *Educational Reform for Disadvantaged Students: An Emerging Crisis* (West Haven, Conn.: National Education Association, 1986), p. 285.
17. Levin, "What Are Accelerated Schools?," p. 1.
18. National Assessment of Educational Progress, *Functional Literacy and Basic Reading Performance* (Washington, D.C.: Office of Education, Department of HEW, 1976).
19. Henry M. Levin, *The Costs to the Nation of Inadequate Education* (Washington, D.C.: Government Printing Office, 1972).
20. Levin, "What Are Accelerated Schools?," p. 3.
21. Ibid., pp. 1–3.
22. Levin, "At Risk Students in a Yuppie Age," p. 292.
23. Levin, *Educational Reform for Disadvantaged Students,* p. 292.

24. Harold Hodgkinson, "Reform vs. Reality," *Phi Delta Kappan,* September 1991, pp. 9–16. (I have drawn on various facets of Hodgkinson's important article.)
25. Ibid., p. 10.
26. Ibid.
27. National Commission on Children, *Beyond Rhetoric,* pp. 18–19.
28. Ibid., p. 33.
29. Ibid., p. 206.
30. Hodgkinson, "Reform vs. Reality," p. 14.

Chapter Nine

1. Lewis, *Restructuring America's Schools,* p. 4.
2. Charles Handy, *The Future of Work: A Guide to a Changing Society* (Oxford: Basil Blackwell, 1985), p. 135.
3. John Dewey, *Problems of Men* (New York: Philosophical Library, 1946), pp. 170–175.
4. John Dewey, *Individualism Old and New* (New York: Capricorn Books, 1962), p. 154.
5. John Dewey, *Intelligence in the Modern World,* ed. Joseph Ratner (New York: Modern Library, 1939), p. 538.
6. John Dewey, *Democracy and Education* (New York: Macmillan, 1916), p. 101.
7. John Dewey, *The Public and Its Problems* (Chicago: Swallow Press, 1954), p. 211.
8. K. C. Cole, "Science Under Scrutiny," *New York Times,* Section 4A, January 7, 1990, p. 18.
9. Ibid.
10. Joseph S. Levine, "Your Child Can Learn Science," *World Monitor,* February 1991, pp. 40–46.
11. Cole, *Science Under Scrutiny,* p. 19.
12. Ibid., p. 21.
13. Ibid., p. 23.
14. Edward B. Fiske, "Reform by High-Tech," *New York Times,* Section 4A, January 7, 1990, pp. 48–49.

Chapter Ten

1. Samuel E. Bleeker, "The Information Age Office," *The Futurist*, January-February 1991, pp. 18-20.
2. Albert Gore, Jr., "Information Superhighways: The Next Information Revolution," *The Futurist*, January-February 1991, p. 23.
3. Darling-Hammond, "Achieving Our Goals," p. 286.
4. David C. Dwyer, Kathy Ringstaff, and Judy Sandholtz, "The Evolution of Teachers' Instructional Beliefs and Practices in High-Access-to-Technology-Classrooms" (Cupertino, Calif.: Apple Computer, 1990).
5. Theodore R. Sizer, *Horace's Compromise: The Dilemma of the American High School* (Boston: Houghton Mifflin, 1984), p. 206.
6. Dwyer and others, "Evolution of Beliefs and Practices," p. 2.
7. Ibid., p. 14.
8. Ibid., pp. 15-16.
9. Ibid., p. 17.
10. Ibid., p. 18.
11. Ibid., p. 21.
12. Ibid., p. 39.
13. Ibid., pp. 25-26.
14. Ibid., p. 29.
15. Ibid., p. 35.
16. Judith Light, "A Study of Technology Transfer from a U.S. Company to the Ministry of Finance of an East African Country." Ph.D. dissertation in process, Washington University, 1992.
17. Reported in Sarason, *The Predictable Failure*, pp. 93-94.
18. David C. Dwyer, "Comments for the National Education Goals Panel." Address delivered in Seattle, Wash., May 8, 1991.

Chapter Eleven

1. Alvin Toffler and Heidi Toffler, "War, Wealth and a New Era in History," *World Monitor*, May 1991, p. 50.

2. Ibid.
3. Ibid., p. 51.
4. See Carl D. Perkins Vocational and Applied Technology Education Act Amendments of 1990; Public Law 101-392 (H.R. 7), September 25, 1990.
5. Roger J. Vaughn, "The New Limits to Growth: Economic Transformation and Vocational Education," *Phi Delta Kappan*, February 1991, p. 428.
6. Nevin R. Frantz, Jr., and Melvin D. Miller, *A Context for Change: Vocational-Technical Education and the Future* (Macomb: Curriculum Publications, Western Illinois University, 1990), pp. 4-7, 49.
7. Ibid., p. 15.
8. William B. Johnston and Arnold H. Packer, *Workforce 2000* (Indianapolis: Hudson Institute, 1987), pp. 97-99.
9. Ibid., pp. 91-92.
10. W. Norton Grubb, *Separating the Wheat from the Chaff: The Role of Vocational Education in Economic Development* (Berkeley: National Center for Research in Vocational Education, 1989), p. 27.
11. Vaughn, "New Limits to Growth," pp. 447-448.
12. Ibid., p. 447.
13. Ibid., p. 446.
14. National Association of Manufacturers, *Proceedings*, 1911, pp. 187-188.
15. Diane Simons, *George Kerschensteiner* (London: Methuen, 1966), p. 30.
16. National Association of Manufacturers, *Proceedings*, 1912, p. 154.
17. Larry Rosenstock, "The Walls Come Down: The Overdue Reunification of Vocational and Academic Education," *Phi Delta Kappan*, February 1991, p. 434.
18. Perkins Act Amendments of 1990. See also John G. Wirt, "A New Federal Law on Vocational Education: Will Reform Follow?," *Phi Delta Kappan*, February 1991, pp. 425-433.
19. See Rosenstock, "The Walls Come Down," pp. 434-436.
20. Ibid., p. 434.

21. L. B. Resnick, "Learning in School and Out," *Educational Researcher,* December 1987, pp. 13–20.
22. Wirt, *A New Federal Law,* p. 428.
23. Ibid., p. 432.
24. "Integrated Studies Program: Thinking About Technology," *M.I.T. Spectrum,* Fall 1990, pp. 2–5.
25. "Creating Cambridge: Rindge School of Technical Arts Ninth Grade Program," Rindge School of Technical Arts, Cambridge Public Schools, 459 Broadway, Cambridge, Mass. (Unpublished, 1991.)
26. Ibid., p. 1.
27. Dewey, *Democracy and Education,* p. 358.
28. See Lewis Feuer, "John Dewey and the Back to the People Movement," *Journal of Ideas* 20 (1959): 567.
29. John Dewey, *Education Today* (New York: Putnam, 1949), p. 48.
30. John Dewey, *Ethics* (New York: Henry Holt, 1908), p. 408.
31. Dewey, *The Public and Its Problems,* p. 175.
32. Dewey, *Individualism Old and New,* p. 133.
33. Dewey, *Ethics,* p. 406.
34. Katherine C. Mayhew and Anna C. Edwards, *The Dewey School* (New York: Appleton-Century-Crofts, 1936), p. 6.
35. John Dewey, *The School and Society* (Chicago: University of Chicago Press, 1923), pp. 131–132.
36. Ibid., pp. 131–132.
37. Dewey, *Democracy and Education,* p. 192.
38. Havel, *Living in Truth,* p. 153.

Chapter Twelve

1. Philip G. Herbst, *Socio-Technical Design* (London: Tavistock, 1974), p. 203.
2. Ibid., pp. 203–204.
3. Ibid., p. 205.
4. Ibid., pp. 205–206.
5. Ibid., p. 208.
6. Ibid., p. 206.

7. Reich, *The Work of Nations,* p. 108.

8. Ibid., p. 109.

9. See "U.S. Students Near the Foot of the Class," *Science,* March 1988, p. 1237.

10. Reich, *The Work of Nations,* p. 208.

11. Bennett Harrison and Barry Bluestone, *The Great U Turn* (New York: Basic Books, 1988), p. 164. See also Reich, *The Work of Nations,* chap. 16, "American Incomes."

12. *St. Louis Post-Dispatch,* May 15, 1991, p. B-1; September 8, 1991, pp. F-1 and G-3.

13. Reich, *The Work of Nations,* p. 207.

14. Quoted in Reich, *The Work of Nations,* p. 60. See Ellwood P. Cubberley, *Public Education in the United States* (Boston: Houghton Mifflin, 1934), p. 527.

15. Meier, "Bush and the Schools," p. 331.

16. National Commission on Children, *Beyond Rhetoric,* p. 24.

17. Reich, *The Work of Nations,* p. 302.

18. Lynn White, *Dynamo and Virgin Reconsidered* (Boston: MIT Press, 1968), p. 25.

19. John Bremer, *A Matrix for Modern Education* (Toronto: McClellan & Stewart, 1975), pp. 11–15.

20. Kalman H. Silvert, *The Reason for Democracy* (New York: Viking Press, 1977), p. 117.

☰ Selected Bibliography ☰

Bailey, Thomas. *Jobs of the Future and the Skills They Will Require.* Berkeley: National Center for Research in Vocational Education, University of California, 1991.

Baker, Falcon. *Saving Our Kids from Delinquency, Drugs and Despair.* New York: HarperCollins, 1991.

Becker, Ernest. *The Structure of Evil: An Essay on the Unification of the Science of Man.* New York: Free Press, 1968.

Bentham, Jeremy. *The Works of Jeremy Bentham.* New York: Russell & Russell, 1962.

Bernstein, Richard J. *Beyond Objectivism and Relativism.* Philadelphia: University of Pennsylvania Press, 1983.

Bleeker, Samuel E. "The Information Age Office." *The Futurist,* 1991, *35* (1), 18–20.

Bremer, John. *A Matrix for Modern Education.* Toronto: McClellan & Stewart, 1975.

Carnoy, Martin, and Henry M. Levin. *Schooling and Work in the Democratic State.* Stanford: Stanford University Press, 1985.

Cole, K. C. "Science Under Scrutiny." *New York Times,* Section 4A, January 7, 1990, p. 18.

Cooley, Mike. *Architect or Bee?* Boston: South End Press, 1981.

Cuban, Larry. *Teachers and Machines: The Classroom Use of Technology Since 1920.* New York: Teachers College Press, 1986.

Cubberley, Ellwood P. *Public Education in the United States.* Boston: Houghton Mifflin, 1934.

Darling-Hammond, Linda. "Achieving Our Goals: Superficial or Structural Reforms?" *Phi Delta Kappan,* 1990, 72 (4), 288-290.

Dewey, John. *Ethics.* New York: Henry Holt, 1908.

Dewey, John. *Democracy and Education.* New York: Macmillan, 1916.

Dewey, John. *Intelligence in the Modern World,* ed. Joseph Ratner. New York: Modern Library, 1939.

Dewey, John. *Problems of Men.* New York: Philosophical Library, 1946.

Dewey, John. *Education Today.* New York: Putnam, 1949.

Dewey, John. *The Public and Its Problems.* Chicago: Swallow Press, 1954.

Dewey, John. *Individualism Old and New.* New York: Capricorn Books, 1962.

Dewey, John. *Liberalism and Social Action.* New York: Capricorn Books, 1962.

Dolce, Danilo. In Cherise Wyneken (ed.), *Touchstones.* Center City, Minn.: Hazelden, 1986.

Domenico, Raymond. *Model for Choice: A Report on Manhattan's District 4.* New York: Manhattan Institute, 1989.

Draper, Robert. "The Golden Arm." *New York Review of Books,* 1985, *32* (6), 46-49.

Dubos, René. *The God Within.* New York: Scribner's, 1972.

Duke, Benjamin. *The Japanese School: Lessons for Industrial America.* New York: Praeger, 1986.

Dyson, Anne Haas. "The Value of 'Time Off Task': Young Children's Spontaneous Talk and Deliberate Text." *Harvard Educational Review,* 1987, *57* (4), 396-420.

Foucault, Michel. *Discipline and Punish.* New York: Vintage Books, 1979.

Frantz, Nevin R., and Melvin D. Miller. *A Context for Change:*

Vocational-Technical Education and the Future. Macomb: Curriculum Publications, Western Illinois University, 1990.

Gadamer, Hans-Georg. *Truth and Method.* New York: Crossroad, 1986.

Goodlad, John. *A Place Called School.* New York: McGraw-Hill, 1984.

Goodman, Kenneth S., and others. *Report Card on Basal Readers.* Katonak, N.Y.: Richard C. Owen, 1988.

Goulet, Denis. *The Uncertain Promise.* New York: IDOC/North America, 1977.

Gray, Kenneth. "Vocational Education in High School: A Modern Phoenix." *Phi Delta Kappan,* 1991, 72 (6), 436–438.

Grubb, W. Norton. *Separating the Wheat from the Chaff: The Role of Vocational Education in Economic Development.* Berkeley: National Center for Research in Vocational Education, 1989.

Handy, Charles. *The Future of Work: A Guide to a Changing Society.* Oxford: Basil Blackwell, 1985.

Harrison, Bennett, and Barry Bluestone. *The Great U Turn: Corporate Restructuring and the Polarization of America.* New York: Basic Books, 1988.

Havel, Vaclav. *Living in Truth.* London: Faber & Faber, 1990.

Hodgkinson, Harold. "Reform vs. Reality." *Phi Delta Kappan,* 1991, 73 (1), 9–16.

Investing in Our Children: Business and the Public Schools. New York: Committee for Economic Development, 1985.

Jaeger, Werner. *Paideia: The Ideals of Greek Culture.* New York: Oxford University Press, 1945.

Johnston, William B., and Arnold H. Packer. *Workforce 2000.* Indianapolis: Hudson Institute, 1987.

Kozol, Jonathan. *Savage Inequality.* New York: Crown, 1991.

Levin, Henry M. *Educational Reform for Disadvantaged Students: An Emerging Crisis.* West Haven, Conn.: National Education Association, 1986.

Levin, Henry M., and R. W. Rumberger. *The Educational Implications of High Technology.* Project Report No. 83–84. Stanford: Institute for Research on Educational Finance and Governance, 1983.

Lewis, Anne. *Restructuring America's Schools.* Arlington, Va.: American Association of School Administrators, 1989.

Luke, Allan. "Making 'Dick and Jane': Historical Genesis of the Modern Basal Reader." *Teachers College Record,* 1987, *89* (1), 91–103.

Meier, Deborah. "Good Schools Are Still Possible." *Dissent,* Fall 1987, pp. 543–549.

Meier, Deborah. "Bush and the Schools: A Hard Look." *Dissent,* Summer 1991, pp. 330–331.

National Commission on Children. *Beyond Rhetoric: A New American Agenda for Children and Families.* Washington, D.C.: National Commission on Children, 1991.

National Commission on Testing and Public Policy. *From Gatekeeper to Gateway: Transforming Testing in America.* Chestnut Hill, Mass.: Boston College, 1990.

Nitobe, Inazo. *The Works of Inazo Nitobe.* Tokyo: University of Tokyo Press, 1969. (Originally published 1900.)

Piaget, Jean. *To Understand Is to Invent: The Future of Education.* New York: Grossman, 1973.

Raywid, Mary Anne. "The Evolving Effort to Improve Schools: Pseudo-Reform, Incremental Reform, and Restructuring." *Phi Delta Kappan,* 1990, *72* (2), 141–142.

Reich, Robert B. *The Next American Frontier.* New York: New York Times Books, 1983.

Reich, Robert B. *The Work of Nations: Preparing Ourselves for 21st Century Capitalism.* New York: Knopf, 1991.

Resnick, L. B. "Learning in School and Out." *Educational Researcher,* 1987, *19* (9), 13–20.

Rosenstock, Larry. "The Walls Come Down: The Overdue Reunification of Vocational and Academic Education." *Phi Delta Kappan,* 1991, *72* (6), 434–435.

Sarason, Seymour B. *The Predictable Failure of Educational Reform: Can We Change Course Before It's Too Late?* San Francisco: Jossey-Bass, 1990.

Silvert, Kalman H. *The Reason for Democracy.* New York: Viking Press, 1977.

Simons, Diane. *George Kerschensteiner.* London: Methuen, 1966.

Sizer, Theodore R. *Horace's Compromise: The Dilemma of the American High School.* Boston: Houghton Mifflin, 1984.

Smith, Mary Lee. "Put It to the Test: The Effects of External Testing on Teachers." *Educational Researcher,* 1991, *20* (5), 9–11.

Toffler, Alvin, and Heidi Toffler. "War, Wealth and a New Era in History." *World Monitor,* 1991, *4* (5), 48–54.

Vaughn, Roger J. "The New Limits to Growth: Economic Transformation and Vocational Education." *Phi Delta Kappan,* 1991, *72* (6), 428–430.

Vermilye, Dyckman W., ed. *Relating Work and Education.* San Francisco: Jossey-Bass, 1977.

Warnke, Georgia. *Gadamer.* Stanford: Stanford University Press, 1987.

"What Is Authentic Evaluation?" *Democracy and Education,* 1990, *5* (1), 17–20.

Wirt, John G. "A New Federal Law on Vocational Education: Will Reform Follow?" *Phi Delta Kappan,* 1991, *72* (6), 425–433.

Wirth, Arthur G. *Education in the Technological Society: The Vocational-Liberal Studies Controversy in the Early Twentieth Century.* Lanham, Md.: University Press of America, 1980. (Originally published in 1972.)

Wirth, Arthur G. *Productive Work in Industry and Schools: Becoming Persons Again.* Lanham, Md.: University Press of America, 1983.

Wirth, Arthur G. *John Dewey as Educator (1894–1904).* Lanham, Md.: University Press of America, 1989. (Originally published in 1966.)

Zuboff, Shoshanna. *In the Age of the Smart Machine: The Future of Work and Power.* New York: Basic Books, 1988.

Index

A

Accelerated Schools Project, 111–116, 205
Ada, A., 27
Adler, M. J., 160
Aldridge, B., 125
Anders, W., 194
Apple Classroom of Tomorrow (ACOT): case studies of two teachers, 141–145; deeper meaning, 147–151; described, 133–146; stages of, 135–140
Ashcroft, J., 90
At-risk students, 111–120
Automate: as work style, 2–3, 41–42, 100, 133

B

Bailey, J., 33
Bartman, R., 91
Basals, described, 14–17; genesis of, 18–19
Becker, E., 9

Bennett, W., 77, 101, 128
Bentham, J.: and panopticon control, 20–21, 85
Bernstein, R., 22
Berryman, S., 35, 99
Bieber, O., 39
Bildung, as self-transformation, 28
Bluestone, B., 193
Boston Women's Teachers' Group, 10–13
Boyer, E., 99
Bremer, J., 207
Bureau of Labor Standards: and job changes, 32
Bush, G., 90
Bushido, Japanese philosophy, 46–47
Business: perspective on educational reform, 71–75, 91
Butler, O., 100

C

CEO's income, 194
Campbell, G., 154